Tiger's Eye: A Memoir

Inga Clendinnen was born in Geelong in 1934. Her books and scholarly articles on the Aztecs and Maya of Mexico have won a number of awards. She is also the author of *Reading the Holocaust* which in 1999 was named as a Best Book of the Year by the *New York Times* and won the New South Wales Premier's General History Award. In 1999 she also delivered the ABC's Boyer Lectures. Her essays and short fiction have been widely published.

BY THE SAME AUTHOR

Ambivalent Conquests: Spaniard and Mayan in Yucatan, 1517–1577
Aztecs: An Interpretation
Reading the Holocaust
True Stories (ABC Boyer Lectures)

Tiger's Eye

A MEMOIR

Inga Clendinnen

JONATHAN CAPE
LONDON

Published by Jonathan Cape 2001

2 4 6 8 10 9 7 5 3 1

Copyright © Inga Clendinnen

Inga Clendinnen has asserted her right under the Copyright, Designs
and Patents Act 1988 to be identified as the author of this work

First published in Great Britain in 2001 by
Jonathan Cape
Random House, 20 Vauxhall Bridge Road,
London SW1V 2SA

Random House Australia (Pty) Limited
20 Alfred Street, Milsons Point, Sydney,
New South Wales 2061, Australia

Random House New Zealand Limited
18 Poland Road, Glenfield,
Auckland 10, New Zealand

Random House South Africa (Pty) Limited
Endulini, 5A Jubilee Road, Parktown 2193, South Africa

The Random House Group Limited Reg. No. 954009
www.randomhouse.co.uk

A CIP catalogue record for this book is available from the British Library

ISBN 0-224-06123-2

Papers used by Random House are natural,
recyclable products made from wood grown in sustainable forests;
the manufacturing processes conform to the environmental
regulations of the country of origin

'Reading Mr Robinson', 'Indians' and 'Lace' first appeared in *Australian Book Review*.
'The Misses Wan' piece first appeared in *Overland*, 'Lillit' first appeared in *Heat* and 'Island' first
appeared in *Voices*.

Printed and bound in Great Britain by Mackays of Chatham plc

CONTENTS

TO ABSENT FRIENDS

I sing of bodies changed into shapes of a different kind.

OVID, *METAMORPHOSES*

A decade ago, when I was in my early fifties, I fell ill. 'Fall' is the appropriate word; it is almost as alarming and quite as precipitous as falling in love. It is even more like falling down Alice's rabbit hole into a world which might resemble this solid one, but which operates on quite different principles. Pain, death and loneliness are domestic presences there, in grey-green masks and gloves. So are humour and kindness, which come in all sorts of uniform. You are granted the dubious privilege of being a child again in a place which sometimes resembles a child's nightmare, and at others a well-run nursery.

It is also a world in which, like Alice, you are subject to unscheduled and surprising transformations.

This is not the story of a medical crisis. If it were, it would be for medicos to write. To lie still as a crusader on a tomb while dreams spin behind closed lids, to surf the tumble of disordered memories as they dolphin away, to feel the mind disintegrate and to fear the disintegration of the self, is to suffer an existential crisis, not a medical one. And to try to understand any of this by transforming inchoate, unstable emotion and sensation into marks on paper is to experience the abyss between fugitive thought, and the words to contain it.

This is the story of what happened when I fell down my rabbit hole.

BEGINNINGS

INTIMATIONS

It began with small things.

My dentist, a friend since student days, prodded my pulpy gums, frowned, and said, 'Inga, I don't like the look of this. This looks systemic.'

I nodded, sagely. Systemic? What could he mean? I had only used that word, I realised, metaphorically. Systemic. Because he looked so solemn, because we are friends, I did not like to ask.

My gums continued to bleed. Blood crusted in my nose, crescents of gummy red. Then a cool dribble. I made a Desdemona handkerchief, spotted all over with strawberries of blood. I used to have nosebleeds, bad ones, as a child, but at my age?

In class, discussing bloodstained Aztecs with my students, my nose began to bleed in steady drops, like placid rain. It bled for five minutes. This group of assorted Australians was puzzling over what a group of assorted Mexicans, once alive, now five hundred years dead, meant by some complicated doings with tongues and obsidian razors and smoothed sticks and cords. What they mainly did was bleed. But who bled, and who was made to bleed? Did those who bled do so voluntarily, and at this distance how could we tell? Therefore a monsoon of jokes accompanied my genteel, chronic dripping-from-the-nose. My students said there would be much rain in Melbourne this season.

The public nose-bleeding happened often. I began to leave bloody fingerprints on books, even on student essays. In class the drips could come so fast that I would have to leave and stand in the toilet until they stopped.

As I walked back to my office one day an older student, who still surrounded me with the conventionalised tenderness of male courtesy, stepped through the invisible ring and said, quietly, 'You should see someone about that.'

The students had gone with the spring. As I trudged the Anglesea beach, the loose happy weight of my grand-daughter's body, not forty months in this bright world, warm against mine, sharing her breath, laughing into her sea-washed eyes, the sand was suddenly thick as glue. My son turned. 'Are you OK?' I made a joke about 'she's not heavy, she's my grand-daughter', as I let her go from me, for the first time willingly. She twisted to look back from his shoulder as he strode away in seven-league bare feet. I pulled a clown's woebegone face, she laughed, grabbed at his hair. Standing, breathing, trembling, thinking, 'This can't be right.'

So I admitted it, like a guilty secret: I was not well. It had been difficult to put these small things together, and to say they made one big thing. My family has always been stoical about ailments. No, not my family. It was my mother who was stoical, and I found she had taught me well. She was stoical about her own ailments, ironic about mine, so I still dread making a fuss about nothing.

When I was a child, even vomiting didn't impress her. There was only one test. She would apply her pursed lips to my forehead, and let them rest there for the space of seven heartbeats. Then, eyes on my face but spirit elsewhere, consulting some other, less contaminated and less anxious source, she would speak. If the invisible thumb pointed up it was to bed with mid-morning lemonade, if down it was off on the long walk to school.

I know now that she was sometimes wrong. I remember being sent home from school an hour after I'd tottered the whole two kilometres there with a raging fever, and the fury of a brother hauled from his classroom to walk me home again. I had to keep sitting down on the nature strip to throw up into the gutter. I remember sitting on a chair in our cool dim kitchen watching my brother's face as it ballooned into a moon and a swarming buzzing darkness poured in through the door and leapt to swallow me. After a tingling sleep I woke, mysteriously under the chair, with a leg bent under me and thinking, 'Whose leg can that be? It's really hurting someone.' That was my first experience of fainting. I've fainted quite often since, but the sinister perturbation of sensation is not something you get used to—although the moment of returning consciousness is so fresh and extraordinary as to make it almost worthwhile.

In the face of experience, my faith remained unaffected: I trusted my mother's lips. I knew that their cool pressure on my forehead would compel the goblins gibbering in my interior to declare themselves. I could not doubt it because I could feel it happening. The few times I was taken on the long walk-and-tram journey into central Geelong to see the Doctor, a silent, toad-like old party squatting deep in a vine-swathed Edwardian mansion, I thought it was just that, a business of setting eyes on him—a ritual pass executed by my mother as part of her plan for my restoration.

My mother the shaman. But the shaman is dead, and these intimations of non-health would not surrender to mid-morning lemonade. In the absence of my mother's lips—what is grief but the lack of particular lips?—I resorted to the rational project of making a list.

My gums bled, my nose bled, I was tired to the point of weeping. Chewing and swallowing took more energy than I had. I was thin, but sometimes my belly was fat, big enough for three babies. I was often dizzy. I had strange buzzing days when I could not concentrate and felt persistently nauseous. Sometimes I had stomach pains. They only lasted for a few minutes, but while they lasted I had to double up, even lie down on the ground, wherever I happened to be.

Set down, it was quite a list. So I took it to my doctor. She listened with the slightly unfocused look of someone not listening, or listening to an echo I could not hear. Bouncing her fingers on the drum of my belly, my extruded navel a gleaming Buddha squatting on the very top of the curve, she diagnosed post-menopausal blues.

I was outraged. I pointed out that I had menopaused with no drama at all the year before, when I was fifty-three, that I did not feel in the least 'blue', that what I did feel was rather sinisterly ill. This squat matronly nincompoop fifteen years my junior gave me a mini-lecture on relinquishing youth gracefully.

It would have been funny were I not so furious.

Now my nose scarcely stopped bleeding, the pains were worse, the fatigue could not be confused with any failure of will. I worked my way through the other doctors in the clinic. They listened with the same glassy opacity. From being a 'good' patient, intelligent, agreeable, docile, I was becoming a very bad patient indeed: argumentative, tart, with an inconveniently precise memory.

My feet, then my ankles, began to swell, so that I could not walk on them and had to hire a wheelchair, and an army of small red spots began marching up my legs. 'Gout,' said the oleaginous senior doctor, but there was a note of interrogation. I could see he was shaken. At last he took a blood test. Not gout. He threw in the towel, sent me to a diagnostic physician, and in ten minutes I had the magic name: Active Auto-Immune Hepatitis. Acute liver disease.

It is a rare illness, identified only in the early eighties. Then it had been a brisk killer, mainly of teenage girls, so what was it doing attacking me? These days, I was told, it could be controlled by drugs—drugs with unfortunate side effects, but which, by and large and for a time, work. By and large. For a time.

The diagnosis was confirmed by tests and a number of small episodes from the last several decades—disabling headaches roaring out of nowhere, Olympian hangovers after two glasses of wine—scuttled into a queue and held up their placards: Active Auto-Immune Hepatitis.

My main feeling was of triumphant vindication: I really was ill. I was also surprised. My family has always died young and cholerically, by heart attack or stroke. I was also obscurely gratified: this was, after all, a new and stylish disease, rare, even dangerous. I was flattered when my specialist sent me over to one of Melbourne's famous institutions, the Walter and Eliza Hall, to have some of my interestingly toxic blood siphoned off for 'research'. It turned out to be arterial blood they wanted, and I did not enjoy the experience, but there I was in among the test tubes and the soft-voiced people in the white coats, pushing away with my mouse shoulder at the frontiers of science. This disease was a kind of distinction. This disease, I privately thought, had class.

The vague and inappropriate jubilation lingered until I was talked to by my specialist, a blessedly direct man in a profession given to silences or circumlocution. He told me that the condition could be stabilised but not cured, that what I was assuming to be a temporary state was permanent, that with luck I would not deteriorate too quickly. My jubilation sagged less because of his words than his regretful tone. This was bad news I was hearing.

What distinguishes the healthy from the ill—which is a more significant division in any society than class or gender or possibly even homelessness—is that the healthy consider feeling well to be the normal state of things. My physical discomforts thus far were trivial, or could seem so for as long as I thought them temporary. But if I were not 'returned to health', if they were permanent, I would presumably have to become some strange new kind of person: an invalid. I had no notion what that person might be like.

My friends began to treat me with touching deference. Twice a day I swallowed drugs by the half-handful. I was given lists of their side effects, which made me laugh because they ran from blindness to cancer. I was soberly assured it was not obligatory to experience them all. This new society of the unwell and their custodians was a solemn one.

The drugs took effect: my nose and gums bled less. But it was, as they say, a trade-off. The drugs made the skin fragile, and weakened the capillary walls; I bruised spectacularly at a touch. If I dropped a page of bond paper it sliced skin; when I filed the sheet the backs of my hands stained purple. I was still leaving bloody fingerprints everywhere like an inept villain, and I was as frightened in the streets as an octogenarian: I dreaded injury, inflicted not by a delinquent on a skateboard but by a toddler on a trike, not by a ravening rottweiler but a sociable puppy. My younger son, a basketballer, bought me a pair of bright turquoise shin-guards. They poked out from the bottom of my slacks. I looked like a blotchily painted tin soldier, but I felt better armed.

I was not wearing them the day I fell over in Kew High Street. I fell hard and downhill, catching my sandal-tip on an uneven pavement I couldn't see for the birthday cake I was carrying in front of me. I fell just beside a tram stop, where a cluster of people, all under twenty-five, were waiting. I lay shocked and winded among my scattered parcels, blood welling out of my knees and arm, rehearsing the brave and reassuring things I would say when someone came to help.

Nobody moved. A young man whose feet were less than two metres from my head stared stonily ahead. I fantasised elbow-crawling over to his legs, clamping my teeth into his calf, and holding on.

Slowly I collected myself, levered myself upright, retrieved the cake (collapsed on impact, dead on arrival) and went home in a state of serious disaffection from well society.

I would see the specialist once a month, and he confirmed my own diagnosis: there was some deterioration. The belly-swelling was especially bad. I had to give a lecture, arranged months earlier, with a loose sweater pulled down over the gaping waistband of my skirt, which, being unfastened, hung nearly to my ankles. I attended a couple of sessions of a conference in the same condition and costume, and was relieved and offended when no-one noticed.

Very occasionally the specialist would mention the possibility of a liver transplant 'somewhere down the track'. His glance was speculative. Later I understood the caution: they had only just begun to do the operation in Melbourne and, despite a new wonder drug, it was still a desperate remedy.

His sentence hung in the air. I had no idea how to respond. The idea seemed preposterously melodramatic.

I was not reconciled to any of this.

After months of pill-swallowing, I was getting sicker.

Over the first twelve years of life bodies change fast. They continue to change, disturbingly, excitingly, for the next ten. And then they settle down. Nothing much changes for the next long while, or nothing we choose to regard as irreversible, until the day when we see an old lady—a long-dead aunt? a fugitive from a nursing home?—walking up the stairs as we are walking down, and we meet in the mirror on the landing.

Now there were too many changes, coming too fast. I had no

sooner been diagnosed by way of my red tide of polka dots than my sedate middle-aged body flung itself into a positive fandango of change. My skin abandoned what I had taken to be its minimal duty of keeping the inside in: it spat and dribbled blood at the mildest affront, the most oblique insult. My skin-scape turned tropical: huge bruises bloomed like orchids, luxuriated for weeks. My belly justified its name, swelling grand as a spinnaker, sagging to a derelict marsupial pouch, then swelling again. The doctors called it 'ascites', and said it was caused by 'the accumulation of fluids'. What fluids? Where? What it looked like was witchcraft.

Meanwhile the rest of my person thinned. Long-buried bones elbowed their way to the surface. I previewed my face at eighty, then eighty years after that: my skull waggled its jawbones at me; my skeleton danced like a witchdoctor under purple skin. Then a diet of steroids obliterated these Boschian portents in a wave of unnaturally thick flesh. My face expanded and took on a threatening flush, my mouth, squashed between swollen cheeks, pursed like a wind-cherub's, my lank hair crisped into a wig of Harpo Marx curls. I had transformed into a choleric kewpie.

Vanity set up a wail, but without conviction. Drugs and disease were only effecting more briskly what the years would have anyway. And, as lovers of volcanos know, radical change is always worth watching. Alice might not have enjoyed her multiple transformations down the rabbit hole, but she never doubted they were adventures, and much to be preferred to a life of Sunday afternoons in her own natural body.

While I could not always match her insouciance, I understood how she felt. I had reached something of a Sunday in my own life. Rather too many people had rather too clear expectations of me, which I had become rather too deft at not, quite, disappointing. The stand-off could have lasted to the grave. Now, clearly, it was over.

Alice also learnt how her changing physical attributes affected the behaviour of the creatures around her, and so did I. The question of gait, for example. I have always moved quickly. This new creature tottered and creaked, and had to be levered out of chairs. My voice changed: once an instrument I enjoyed playing, it thinned to a reedy whisper. Things said in this shreddy little voice roused pity in some, embarrassment in others, a mixture of both in most. I had become very visibly an invalid, and the recipient of the standard negative emotions—distaste, resentment, dread—that invalids elicit, along with a few more charitable ones. My moods were constantly misread: trivial irritations were heard as confessions of despair, ordinary ironies as heroic. When I tried to point any of this out I would be told, through words or intonation, that I was being very, very brave; when I reacted grumpily, I was soothed.

What to do? My old panoply of self-representing devices was in full mutiny. To continue to be 'myself', whoever that might be, I would have to do some systematic thinking. To do that, I needed to write.

I have always had trouble making sense of things—road signs, machines, maps—but also human fears, obsessions and motivations, including my own. It is largely through the sustained internal talking which gives rise to words on the page that I discover what I am thinking and feeling: in the larger sense, what is going on. While it has been something of an impediment in life, my capacity for bafflement made me a good historian. Incapable of taking anything at face value, I would peer so long and anxiously at bits and pieces surviving from the past that I could sometimes discern shapes and patterns that other, brisker people had overlooked.

Now writing took on a new urgency. I had watched my body, an old and, as I had thought, staunch comrade, changing shape as casually as any shaman. While I was impressed by its transformations, even beguiled by its unsuspected flair for melodrama, its defection left me lonely. Illness also isolated me socially. Now I lived behind the invisible cordon of the chronically unwell.

More disturbing were what seemed to be changes inside my head. My memory was beginning to slip. An object would be mislaid, a familiar name forgotten. A commonplace word, like 'cupboard' or 'glass', would obstinately elude my tongue. I learnt that the liver is an extraordinary organ with a finger in every pie; that when it malfunctions toxins leak into the brain, and that these toxins affect the mind. So I began making lists, and losing them, looking up words, and forgetting them, using endearments to avoid naming names. Conversations became difficult—I would lose the theme—and the tempo was broken, because my mind was slowing. Not long before, it had moved with reasonable speed. Now it was a sluggish pond, with obscure shapes blundering around on the muddy bottom. Only through writing could I hope to identify those shapes; to develop a slower, muddier interior conversation with my slower, muddier self.

And then, towards the end of the first year of my illness, with no more warning than a sudden fever, wild coughing and total debility, I was projected with septicaemia and liver failure into Intensive Care in a large public hospital. I was dangerously ill, and hallucinating freely. After a week I graduated to the acute medical ward, where the hallucinations continued, but were challenged by a frail returning sense of self.

IN A TIGER LANDSCAPE

While frightening, the hallucinations did not seem particularly sinister, because I had an explanation for them. I decided they were an exhausted mind's attempt to make sense out of random visual phenomena, 'phosphenes', I thought they were called: the specks and flashes of light stimulated in the eye or the brain by pressure or some other physical disturbance. I had read that phosphenes provided the raw physiological material for the collective dream-journeys taken by certain Amazonian Indians after ingesting hallucinogenic drugs. What did surprise me was that mine organised themselves so exotically. What I saw were *wayan kulits*, Balinese shadow-puppet plays, enacted in blood and fire against the curtains drawn around my bed, along with tamer single-line processions of small red turtles and large red cockroaches which scuttled across the floor, up the walls, across the ceilings, down the walls, across the floor and up the walls again.

Even at the time I grasped that these bizarre visuals had a lot to do with the old woman in the bed next to mine. She was quite mad, muttering in an urgent, unintelligible whisper, and every single night she would struggle to get up and over the high metal bars penning her into her cot. In the vague light I would see her agitated shadow projected onto the curtain between us, skinny legs twisting, skinny arms semaphoring, skinny body lurching and flapping. Then the shadow would be swallowed in a larger darkness and violently shaking fabric—and she would erupt through the curtains to pounce on my feet, or rattle the bars of my cot, or rummage in the metal drawer by my head. I was terrified of her and wished her dead, even when with each dawn I would watch her shrink to demented pathos again.

The one truly malevolent hallucination from that time came in full daylight. My older son and his family had come to visit me. My grand-daughter, now close to four years old and the light of my life, was hanging over the bed, fascinated by my transformation and characteristically quite undaunted by it. My son was beside her, and over by the window my daughter-in-law, her face half-obscured by her warm fall of hair, was suckling their baby son.

I was watching the mother and child, sucking in great draughts of comfort from that loveliest of sights, when a tide of blood surged up and obliterated their faces. I looked at my grand-daughter, and saw her small bright face was a mask of blood too. My son was, blessedly, unaffected. It was all I could do to conceal my panic. I shut my eyes, feigned exhaustion, got them safely out of that terrible place—and then yielded, helplessly, to superstitious terror.

In time the effect of that urgent invitation to superstition wore off, and I was able to set aside this very direct threat to sanity. After all, the melodramas of my dream-life were notoriously florid. I was always having visions of near-hallucinatory clarity on waking out of dreams, usually of murderous assaults against family members. In one, that same son was a baby again and being dragged from his bassinette by an obscenely bald and naked man who had inserted half his bloated person under the mosquito net, and who seemed impervious to my homicidal exertions with a huge kitchen knife. In another dawn I sat up in bed to find a late-eighteenth-century firing squad in full military fig, three standing, three kneeling, antique guns levelled, and all of them aiming at my sleeping husband and my goggling self. Unfettered imagination is its own punishment. My 'ordinary' dreams were by contrast wearyingly banal, revelatory of nothing at all, their symbolism so exiguous as to be insulting. My Hidden Dramatist chose not to put himself out. Most of the time I would simply dream, with shocking directness, what needed to be dreamed to get the dream-work done.

Courage was possible in daylight. When night came I had no defence. I was seriously ill, on the lowest level of the rabbit warren. I was frightened. I also discovered I was a claustrophobe. The ward was on the ground floor, but for all my time there I experienced it as underground, a sealed-off place of metal and plastic and rubber and reverberating, sound-gulping silence.

The ward was also adrift in time. Patients around me had strange, archaic diseases. The woman in the bed diagonally opposite had gangrene. She whimpered when they changed her dressings in the morning, a high, continuous whimper, like an animal in a trap.

For the evening dressing she was silent. I think by then she was too exhausted to cry.

I had wasted badly, my bones pressing hard on my skin, so I developed bedsores. I thought bedsores didn't happen any more. Too weak to hold a book, it seemed I couldn't hold a thought in my head, except the thought that I would almost certainly die in there.

The nights were worst. The silence of a hospital in deep night is not real silence. It is a low steady humming with the echoes of all the sounds swallowed during the day thick in it, like the throbbing mechanical silence deep in the bowels of a great ship, where you know you will never be able to find your way up and out to the air. And, of course, there were the hallucinations and the crazy woman in the bed next to mine.

Then one night as I lay watching the curtain shake and the frantic red shadows gibber and gesticulate, I heard a natural sound. It took me long moments to identify it, because it was so surprising. Lions. The zoo lions, roaring. I had forgotten that the hospital was separated from the zoo only by a stretch of parkland.

In a trice I was through the walls, skimming over the dreaming grass, the ghostly trees, the high brick wall and into the zoo. And there were the lions, lolling in their grassy enclosure, complaining to the same moon they had complained to in Africa.

I have always loved zoos, in part for their melancholy—the lonely sailors on shore leave, the lonely old ladies smiling at other people's children, the animals, wrongfully imprisoned, waiting for an explanation. The apes, gloomily masturbating, puzzling as to how their descendants could have turned out so badly. I knew every path and turn of that zoo, and now in the night I walked them.

The recovered zoo reminded me of a game I used to play when I was a child and in my bed at night. Someone had read me a story about a man whose eyes were stolen by a wizard. He could have them back again, the wizard said, if he could find them in the wizard's pile of eyes. So the wizard led him (he was blind, of course) to the heap, and left him to fossick through it.

I don't remember whether he found his eyes or not. It was the search I liked, because as he tried the eyes he could see what that particular animal would see. A wolf's eyes, and he saw flying snow and tossing pelts and blood on grey muzzles. A jaguar's eyes, and he saw deer flinch and start away, the birds fall silent, the jungle hush. Then bears, sharks, hawks, hummingbirds, ants—he tried them all, and I imagined them all.

I envied him, in spite of the fix he was in. It must have been a fine thing, to see all he saw. Now, listening to the lions, rummaging in the memory cupboard of childhood, I found the eye-pile again, and in the empty hours I would reconstruct, in finest detail, some of the worlds the man might have seen. My mind was slow, so I often chose to be a fish or a squid, even a mussel, but species-travel happily filled the hours.

And then deep in my mind I heard a sound I had forgotten, or had not needed to remember until then. Not quite a sound, more a dark crimson vibration, a sensation in the diaphragm: the low, rumbling, sighing cough of the tiger.

He was my favourite beast, because he was the only animal who did not acknowledge he was in a cage. He would pace its length, the huge body moving smooth as a oiled machine, head carried low and level, searchlight eyes absolutely steady, and then at the corner would come the lunging pivot, the blinding turn within the single body length, and he would be padding back the other way, his indifferent gaze sweeping bars, lawns, people, keepers, and dismissing them utterly. Incidents in a tiger landscape.

The vision of the tiger offered me salvation. I too was in a cage, with feeding times and washing times and bars at the sides of my cot, and people coming to stare and prod, but the kaleidoscope of the horror of helplessness ceased to turn because I withdrew my consent from it. Thereafter, whenever I felt the threat of the violation of self, I would invoke the vision of the tiger and the freedom that vision gave me, to be at once the superb gaze, and the object of the gaze: an incident in a tiger landscape.

It sounds like a religious experience. It was not. It came with no moral or metaphysical messages attached, and it had nothing to do with the supernatural. It was, I think, aesthetic. The tiger emancipated me from the terror of shrivelling death by the beauty and the completeness of his natural being.

INITIATIONS

After about a fortnight I was discharged into the rehabilitation section of a private hospital and the lonely peace of a private room, and over the next couple of months I learnt to feed myself and to walk again. My husband and sons would take me to the park in a wheelchair, it was a beautiful spring, and I experienced the conventional, incomparable joys of convalescence, new-born to the play of light on leaves, of wind on skin, to the shouting birds. The joy of that adult baptism, that re-immersion in the radiance of the natural world, never wears off. And there was a big hydrotherapy pool in the hospital, which renewed my passion for immersion in water.

There was also a bad legacy: a noticeable deterioration in psychological and emotional control. Thereafter, like Sweet Alice Benbow, and when in fact not much moved at all, I would weep at a smile or a frown or (only once, and by mistake) a sneeze. They say this surfeit of sensibility is a consequence of physical weakness. It angered and embarrassed me, and was distressing to my friends.

As soon as I could sit up in the rehabilitation hospital I settled to scribbling on a fat notepad, to find my self and my life again. When I was put into hospital once more, this time for a sequence of tests designed to reveal my increasingly enigmatic internal state, I knew I needed to comprehend this place which I could no longer regard as a place of crisis or of transition, where I was not an occasional visitor, but which would be, for a time at least, my place.

The first thing I had to accept was that hospitals are subversive of all psychological, social and ideological security. You are summoned to hospital, and you go. Everything which follows follows because of that initial submission, which once taken cannot be rescinded. At every later moment you have to remind yourself: 'I chose this.'

The warning signs are everywhere. Admission is by way of wind-scoured plains littered with orphaned cars. Great doors eye you glassily, pause to reflect, decide, gape, you step inside—and you are swallowed sure as any Jonah. Immutable insideness establishes itself: the too-clean corridors with their untracked polished floors, empty waiting rooms, closed doors with cryptic signs on them. The windows behind the venetian blinds are sealed. The flowers tottering in the hospital jam jars are moribund amputees. All living plants and all creatures save humans and their attendant germs are exiled to the other side of the glass.

Social trappings are surrendered along with clothes and other valuables at the door of the ward. Abruptly naked, you are thrust into a vestigial smock. Starched, snowy, it rises high to the chin, but stops, incredibly, at the crutch, and at the back the little ties end with the ribcage. When you move, your buttocks show. It is at once lewd and sexless, an outfit designed for depraved choirboys. When you climb into the bed the bottom sheet strikes cold on bare skin; you feel thick rucked stuff under you, and chill with forgotten shame: rubber sheeting.

Then you are labelled. It is unnerving to be tagged around the wrist, more unnerving to be tagged around the ankle as well, as if you might come unstuck and they will have to match up the parts. Now you are a body on one of eight high metal beds. Lying under stiff sheets, eyes fixed on the door, feeling the rubbery chill, you are four years old again.

People come and go; you learn their comings and goings. Your flesh learns to flinch from metal and the bitter kiss of needles. There is no other flesh to comfort it. Carnal contact with your many handlers only parodies intimacy. Too often it also means pain.

Death visits from time to time, but without emotion and uncere-
moniously, its most enduring legacy the tang of methylated spirits
left in the air when the bed has been emptied, stripped and
scrubbed. An hour later and there is another body in the bed,
another label on the wall, and the astringent tang has gone.

Meanwhile, I wrote. I was in a big mixed ward and discovered
when I pulled out my writing pad that in such a ward writing is
'letter-writing', and therefore a collective activity. Topics and items
of local interest were offered by patients and by nursing staff. If
I said, defensively, that I was writing stories, passing strangers—
chaplains, orderlies, tea-ladies—would stop to empty a bucket
of tales about their dogs or their ex-wives over me, or would say
that they were writers too, or would be when they could get
around to it. When they weren't too busy living.

So I brought in my heavy-calibre weapon, my laptop. Its quiet
grey presence, its familiar weight on my knee, its gentle ping of
reproof when I did something foolish, laid a memory-trace of my
old life over the hospital procession of meals, medications, procedures, inspections and unquiet dreaming sleeps. It tossed up joke
phrases and comic misspellings when my mind went dim and my
fingers tottery. It was also a mighty defender against intruders. Not
many people dare to interrupt the laptop tapper. Even the nurses,
even the doctors, faltered: 'Would she dare write about me?'

I would, and I was.

There are rules governing what the sociologists would call
Interinmate Interaction in the public hospital ward. Public wards
contain six to eight beds. What distinguishes male wards is that

male wards talk. First names are exchanged immediately, and used ostentatiously thereafter. From the coughing and hacking of the dawn there rises a swelling roar of talk which mutes a little for the hour after the paper comes, and then drones on until lights out and obligatory silence. Those too ill to participate directly do so by proxy, because their neighbours speak for them: 'Bill here used to play for Warragul, didn't you Bill?' 'Bill here is a Hawk man, aren't you Bill?' 'Bill here used to work up that way, didn't you Bill?'

They do not mention families, except for offhand, curiously shy references to 'the wife', as in 'The wife will be in this afternoon', or bragging about a son's athletic prowess—always a son, never a daughter, and always sport, with the bragging discreet but persistent as a mosquito's whine. They say where they come from and what they do, with the odd yarn and some deliberately soft-focus talk about politics thrown in. They don't want to offend. The aim is solidarity.

To my knowledge—limited, I admit, to what I could glean when parked on a trolley in the hallway or otherwise lurking about—they do not talk about sex, either in deference to the nurses, to whom they exhibit a touching courtesy, or through some more comprehensive delicacy. And the talk has a strangely archaic flavour, as if I were eavesdropping on conversations of my father's generation. I was in Medical sometimes, Surgical sometimes, and nearly all the inmates were over fifty. Would it have been different in Spinal, where nearly everybody is young? Most of these men came from the country or the more remote suburbs. Would city men be different, and where were they? Stowed away in private hospitals? Do city people have better health insurance than country people? Have we changed less than we think? Or do we perhaps revert? What these men shared were old-fashioned virtues—private stoicism, public fellowship.

Women's wards work differently. There are a few two-bed wards, where the fact that two women are lying in bed being waited on calls up such potent images of luxurious sociability that even the seriously unwell feel obliged to attempt the amenities of social intercourse. This is gruesomely exaggerated in private hospitals, where nurses insist on a mood of Great White Ship sprightliness, regardless of the condition of their prostrate passengers.

The more usual situation is that six to eight women, strangers to each other, frightened, often in pain, always at a loss, find themselves lying parallel or foot to foot in a single enclosed space.

Despite the male conviction that women are ferocious talkers, all-women wards are silent places. Very occasionally an older patient might assume the role of mother, introduce herself and solicit the names of her ward companions, but the introductions are formal, with only unmarried women under about twenty-five being introduced by their first names: for the rest it is Miss Carswell, Mrs Johnson, Mrs Phillips and so on.

Where there is no motherly type the silence can last for days. Then during one of the minor routine flusters—the paper round, tea-trolley time—there will be a kindly gesture towards a temporary absentee, whether dozing, or Gone for Tests, so that when she returns she will find the tea with milk and one sugar on her tray alongside her preferred newspaper. There will be explanations, thanks, a flurry of general talk. And silence again. A little conversation might bubble up during meals, but most women prefer to pretend they are alone on their blue-curtained islands.

During the interludes of talk the women will tell each other where they live, and the ages, sexes and present locations of every one of their children and, if they have them, their grandchildren, but very little else. They never say what ails them. In the men's wards diseases and operations are discussed in detail, and people go off to procedures or theatre to a chorus of 'Good on yer, mate, you'll be right', and the talk will be respectfully subdued until the lost mate is trundled back, and his body, whatever its state of sentience, triumphantly welcomed. Women behave as if their maladies were state secrets. I could lie beside someone for a fortnight hearing every detail of the 'private' conversations she conducted with her doctors and kin a metre away from me, and still remain officially ignorant of what was wrong with her.

I learnt most about my ward companions when we ran into each other lined up on trolleys outside Radiology, or up in the gym feebly pulling levers, or sitting in dressing-gown and slippers in the tiny hospital coffee shop, pretending we were elsewhere. In these foreign places we recognised each other as comrades. In time I came to count two women as friends because our individual paths outside the ward crossed often enough to let us abrogate the ward taboos, and to talk like humans.

I don't know whether the men's ward conviviality generated enduring friendships, but on the whole I doubt it. Now I think that in the face of too many simultaneous threats we had simply reverted to life-in-the-cave ways, the men busy forging their hunting-band bonds and the women guarding their family space, even though that space was reduced to a bed and the half-metre of floor around it.

There were, of course, exceptions. When I had been moved to a single room a quiet man from the country spent a few nights in its tiny annexe as a refugee from the men's ward: 'Mag mag mag all day and half the night, I couldn't stand it.' But it is the mixed wards where things can go badly wrong. One well-heeled old woman, deaf, terminally spoilt, sustained a barrage of complaints and intrusive questions to staff and patients alike through all her waking hours, which were long because she had very little wrong with her—an infected ingrown toenail, something like that. She was bitterly resented, even hated, but this was signalled only by thinned lips and slowed responses. No-one told her to shut up or risk being smothered by her own pillow. She was protected by the heroic courtesy of the genuinely ill.

Even without renegades, mixed wards are awkward places. It would seem that being ill and having to live among strangers in a tiny space controlled by an arbitrary and absolute authority is about as much as most of us can manage. When some of the strangers are of the opposite sex, our culture-making energies can fail us altogether. I have seen people, both men and women, so humiliated by their situation—having to defecate, for example, within the hearing of unknown others—that they fall into a trance of misery. One young Turkish man was rendered speechless by the chagrin of knowing that unknown females were witness to his downfallen state, and that some of these unknown females, a few of them young, would handle his body. There were no male nurses, or not enough, there was no room in an all-male ward, his operation was scheduled, he had to stay. So he lay in his bed, and wept. There was also a hospital myth which might have been true about a wild-eyed, wild-haired man who lurched out of the anaesthetic and immediately grabbed at the girl hovering over him, and kept on grabbing all his female nurses thereafter. Did he think he had died and gone to Paradise? As no-one knew what language he spoke, no-one could disabuse him.

In my own mixed ward I was coping with the attentions of a passionate male talker in the bed next to me. Con the Greek grandfather brought no books or magazines with him to hospital, and he bought no newspapers once inside. His English was probably not up to it, in spite of his thirty years in Australia, but I doubt he was much of a reader anyway. Instead he had the television, which he turned on at 6 a.m. and turned off when the nurses finally got around to making him, at 11 p.m. or midnight or later. It didn't matter what the program was, so long as it was noisy, with lots of ads. He didn't watch it. He just needed company because he was miserably, desperately lonely. He needed the warmth of the family hive. Without it he was as desolate as a lost child.

Like a lost child, he had no confidence in the future. His whole family—wife, son, daughter-in-law, the three grandkids living at home, the households of two other sons, plus assorted brothers and sisters, nephews and nieces—would come to visit him every single night, trickling in in ones and twos and family groups until there was a great chattering flock of them. There was meant to be a limit of two visitors per patient, but Anglo-Saxon anti-familism went down before Greek pro-familism with no resistance at all. The adults would jostle and bicker for a spot on the bed and commandeer every available ward chair, and if they had to they sat in rows on the floor, while the children wandered around goggling at the funny people in the other beds. In time (the television still blaring) they'd be settled, but still bobbing about like a mob of starlings in a roosting tree. And there they would stay, every last one of them, down to the smallest nursling, for at least an hour beyond the end of the official visiting time.

At last there would be stirrings and perturbations somewhere in the centre of the flock, a fluttering and a shifting, and the whole congregation would rise in a flapping of scarves and overcoats and a clamour of farewell cries, and move in a body out through the door and down the corridor to the lift.

And Con would be left, sitting bolt upright in his bed, his whole body yearning after the departing hubbub until it was ended by the clang and whoosh of the lift. Then this small, beautiful Greek man with his fierce moustache would shrink, and droop, and collapse into a fretful misery unrelieved until the outriders of the flock would come winging in with the sunset the next day.

The loneliness of the long hospital night unmanned him altogether. The first night he slept for a few hours, but then his light clicked on, and I lay listening to him groaning, muttering, flinging himself about, then ringing furiously for the night nurse: he had a stomach-ache. The next night it was a toothache, the next a mysterious burning sensation in his legs. The nurses were no comfort at all—they'd just give him a Panadol and go away, and if they found him wandering around the corridors they would chase him back to bed. I think the emptiness of the corridors frightened him anyway: I'd hear the agitated feet patter out into the passage, then silence for perhaps half a minute, and then he would come scurrying back to his half-familiar bed. There would be a lot of heavy nose breathing, the double thump as he shook off his slippers, the sound of stiff hospital sheets being ripped back— and then, after the briefest pause, the blue flicker and mutter of the television.

One night I made a mistake: I crawled painfully (and illegally) out of bed to draw my curtains against that infuriating flicker. After that whenever Con was wakeful I'd hear his sibilant Greek hiss, and whether I pretended to be asleep or not he'd be around the curtain and perched on the bed, talking hard against the dark, until the night nurse would notice and give him a lecture and bustle him off to his own bed. And then, ten minutes later, I'd hear the hiss, and he'd be back. He was a gentle and kindly man, but despair dissolves good manners.

One especially bad night when he'd been in and out for what seemed like hours I was tempted to move over and pull back the bedclothes and tell him to hop in. All he needed was a bit of physical contact; he'd told me he had never been separated from his wife for a single night since he was eighteen—but the thought of the ructions when the morning shift found our two grey heads on the one pillow put me off. Come to think about it, mine would be hanging over the side. Con was sure to be a selfish sleeper.

Con drove us all mad, but while we were glad to see him go we all liked him, and when he went we missed him. After all, his only offence was being a loving man, though it was hard to keep that in mind at three o'clock in the morning with the demented moustachioed toddler on the loose.

Gavan was a greater test both of our tolerance and of the mixed-ward system. Gavan was not abashed by his situation, and Gavan didn't abide by any rules. He couldn't afford the time: he was only 'in' for three days, for his regular battery of tests. I first saw him when I was wheeled back from a procedure: a still, flat shape in the bed foot to foot with mine. 'Good,' I thought, 'he looks really sick. He'll be quiet.' When I saw that his eyes had opened, and thinking he might be disoriented (Gavan disoriented!) I looked up from my book and, making clear by my tone that this was a purely formal inquiry, asked him how he was feeling.

He jerked upright like a jack-in-the-box, fixed me with a glittering eye and answered with an exhaustive, detailed and repellent account of his medical history since the second week in April 1984, when he'd had both knees replaced, as he put it, closely followed by his first major episode of bleeding from the bowel. His epic battle with his body obsessed him, and what he demanded was an audience. He was the Ancient Mariner of physical catastrophe. He even had the equivalent of an albatross: whenever he got out of bed he dragged his little yellow oxygen tank behind him like a brow-beaten terrier.

Do you remember the British comedy series called 'Ripping

Yarns'? One of them pivoted around a macabre creation called 'Uncle Jack', an affable old party in an advanced stage of physical decay. He suffered, gloriously, from most known diseases—leprosy, Barcoo rot, plague, tuberculosis, assorted cancers—together with a lot of unknown ones as well. Uncle Jack had a high, reedy, exultant voice. So did Gavan. Uncle Jack was proud of every last sign and symptom of decrepitude. So was Gavan. Uncle Jack, despite his ailments, was a generous and affectionate fellow, reserving the sight of his most disgusting lesions for the delectation of his enraptured nephew. ('Do you want to see my carbuncle?') Gavan was neither generous nor affectionate.

Like many obsessives, he had never really grasped the fact that other people exist. And he had something else Uncle Jack lacked: an autodidact's passion for arcane medical terminology. He was determined that the world at large should be aware of the baroque complexity of his medical condition, and that required a baroque vocabulary. While Uncle Jack was content to use ordinary if luridly descriptive terms for his multiple diseases, Gavan revelled in medical esoterica.

He also cast himself as a fellow professional with the white-coated professionals who ran the hospital. When the specialists and their attendants would come sweeping into the ward with the charge sister, meek as a nun, bringing up the rear, Gavan would be waiting. To the desultory inquiry of 'And how are you, Mr Errr?' he would reply in fulsome, jargon-sodden detail. When the medicos tried to discuss his condition he would interject with suggestions as to possible new drugs and strategies, while the white-coated ones eyed him fishily and failed to cut him out of the conversation.

He wore his wasted body like a banner, at once map and record of his autobiography, and of the epiphanies and catastrophes inherent in Advanced Medical Science. Once, he confided, he had been an ordinary kind of chap. Now he had, or was in process of having, arthritis, septicaemia, one heart attack and possibly two, a stroke and, as I said, a great number of bowel bleedings and blockages. A large piece of his bowel had been excised, which desperate remedy, he carolled joyously, 'hadn't done the trick'. He was deeply jealous of me: potential transplant patients rank high in the catastrophe stakes, and are admitted to some esoteric procedures whose pleasures he had not yet tasted.

We heard every detail of his own procedures, stunningly invasive as they always were. His descriptions took on particular fire when I was about to be trundled off to undergo the same one. We also heard about his singular response to every known drug, the wonder he excited in the most hardened doctors ('they marvel at me,' he'd say, radiant), the awe of students as they read even the condensed version of his medical history and were permitted to look upon his body and to thrust their hands into his wounds.

He was an indolent, demanding, exploitative patient. As befitted the star of the engrossing hospital melodrama which was his life, he appropriated all possible perquisites, taking over the ward radio for private use, playing it from 6 a.m. to 11 p.m., demanding all possible services, exacting all possible privileges. Every morning he would send hard-pressed nurses out to scrounge a *Herald Sun* from some less frugal patient, and then fail even to glance at it.

And he talked: endlessly. If I was reading, he talked. If I was writing, he talked. If I was tapping away at my laptop, he talked. If I struggled out of bed to close my curtains—a direct insult, the ward equivalent of the glove across the face, and a gross violation of ward protocols ('Curtains to be Drawn Only by Nurses and Medical Staff')—and hid in my little blue igloo, he talked to the curtains. He boasted that he had already used up two megabytes of the hospital computer, that his medical record ran to ten volumes. He recounted to the whole ward the epic Christmas Day when in the very thick and marrow of a family party his sphincter collapsed. Gavan had never read Thurber.

Nobody liked him. I know I hated him. He had three daughters living in Melbourne, and not one of them ever came to see him. I think he had no friends at all. He was nonetheless a supremely happy man, grinning like a gargoyle from his chosen perch at death's door.

The last time I saw Gavan he was rolling down the corridor on a trolley, a young orderly pushing him, an attentive nurse at his head. His reedy voice was piping away, and he was clutching volume eleven of his medical history to his concave chest. He was decrepit, and only notionally human, but he exuded the thin reek of a dreadful immortality. I knew then that Gavan would never die.

CHILDHOOD

HERBIE

Sometimes, lying awake among sleeping strangers, I would try to remember the shape of my childhood bedroom and how I had sometimes lain awake then, and what I used to think about to cheer myself up. That was how I remembered Herbie, and my first conscious experience of joy.

Every day except weekends there'd be a long ring on the doorbell just before lunch, and my mother and I would go down the hall and open the door and the baker would be there with his basket on his hip, and the basket filled with loaves of all sorts of bread, long and thin, high and wide, and all smelling warm and sweet. My mother would lean over and pick one out and give him some coins from her limp black purse with the metal clasp while I ran down the steps and took the bunch of thistles I'd collected for Herbie out of the bucket to carry it dripping out the gate to hold for him.

Herbie would swing his great oblong head and I would see his eyes, shining like dark water, and around them the shadows of lashes stiff as reeds, and in the very centre of each a tiny image of me in there too. Sometimes I had clover for him, and the long velvet lip would tweak it delicately out of my hand, and if it were an apple the lip would stretch and curl back and the yellow teeth would pick it up and leave a green question mark of slime in my palm in return. Herbie's breath was sweet as grass. Even the wide band of sweat under his collar and striping the brown wall of his shoulder smelled sweet.

I really only knew his head: the rest of him was too big to see, a mass of bone and muscle and long snaking veins. He would stand and chew, and I would stand and stare into the mirror of his eye. I could see everything in there—the sky, the tree, even the houses on either side. Then the baker would whistle and he'd lift his head and stride—me holding his cheekstrap, jogging beside him—three houses down, while the baker's feet darted and circled and then 'Ho Herb!' and his big shoulders would thrust and the cart would lurch forward, and I would watch him stride off down the hill. Then I would go back to the house to eat the bread he had brought for me.

There were ordinary animals in the street, cats and dogs and a couple of cockies, and sometimes at first light when the room's shapes floated and rearranged themselves and I swung between sleep and waking there'd be a faint hollow pattering in the distance, and I would hear a man's quiet voice, a dog panting, a creak of leather, and I'd know a river of ghost-grey sheep from the green hills on the other side of the bridge was flowing quietly up the street to the saleyards in North Geelong. When it was light I would go out to the gate and there would be the scatter of little dark pellets which were the only sign of their passing. The farm still came to the town in those days. Sometimes as the sun was coming up cattle would roar by like a passing storm, with dogs barking and whips cracking and shouts and curses as they crashed into fences and buffeted gates, and people would come running out of their houses in their dressing-gowns talking and complaining and shaking their heads, and looking up the empty street to see where they had gone. But no-one bothered to come out for Herbie, who came like a god with his bounty, who accepted my offerings like a king, whose eyes held the world.

Then I was five and going to school, and I didn't see Herbie any more. By the time I'd walk the two kilometres home at lunchtime it would be nearly half-past twelve, the bread would be cool on the table, and I'd eat a sandwich and drink my milk and start going back again.

For the first weeks the walk felt very long: the little rise from home, then the long slow fall to the street with the trams, then steeper until the land flattened and there was the clutter of the red school buildings and the dusty peppercorn trees. The walk back was uphill but it always seemed shorter because there was home at the end of it.

Then one day going back to school at lunchtime I'd just got to the top of the first rise when I heard a jingling and Herbie's cart pulled up, and the baker called out, 'Hop in, I'll give you a lift. Got to go back to the bakery, run out of viennas, would you believe it?' I managed to hoist one foot up on to the high springy side board, and then his big red hand came over and hauled me in, and I thumped into the narrow seat, there was Herbie's vast behind, the baker clicked his tongue and shook the reins, and we were off.

Herbie's ears flicked forward. I grabbed for the side rail; suddenly the cart was rocking and plunging. The baker grinned. 'Didn't know old Herbie had it in him, did you? He thinks he's going home. Ah, but he's a grand old boy, aren't you, Herb?' I could only nod and hang on as Herbie's big haunches pumped and the bells jingled and we bounced and bounded down the hill.

We crossed the road with the trams and there was the big slope ahead, and Herbie pumped faster and we were flying now, the baker whistling and sitting light and easy but with his foot braced hard against the front board and Herbie's ears shaking in time with the bells and his big thudding feet. And then, still flying, he arched his tail high so I could see the puckered hole in his bottom stretching into a vertical grin and spilling out great smoking golden gobbets that bounced and flew on the road and left a golden trail behind us, and I was laughing and the baker was laughing and Herbie's ears were shaking, and we pulled up at the school gate and I leapt down and strode into the schoolyard and Herbie and the baker jingled away.

I saw Herbie, years later, beribboned and jaunty, pulling his elegant fresh-painted cart at the Geelong Show, the reins held by his friend the baker, together still and both of them happy. May they rest well.

THE MISSES WAN

In hospital the mornings are always busy. We would grumble about them—'always at you, won't give you a moment to catch your breath'—but we preferred them to the long, hollow afternoons, when nothing happens at all. The nurses would pull up the pale blue quilts and tuck us in tight and vanish into the nurses' room, where their gusts of laughter reminded us that these cool young creatures on whom our lives depended had their real lives elsewhere.

The afternoons were for visitors, but nobody came. Most of the patients were old or from the country, most were in for long stays, so what visitors there were would dash in on their way home from work wrapped in their envelopes of fresh cold air, or drift in late on Sundays when the afternoon was over and the evening not yet begun: a time between, only fit for visiting aunts. Yes, we noticed. Yes, we resented it. We'd like to say, 'You only come when it suits you, what do you think it's like for us, stuck in here all day?' But we didn't say it. We wouldn't risk it. If we did they might not come at all.

On one of those hollow afternoons I fell into a doze. When I woke there was a tiny bouquet, bound with grass and no bigger than my thumb, stuck into the medicine glass on the tray: a wisp of thyme, three forget-me-nots, a blurred blue daisy, a lantana flower. I could see each bush of the little front garden they had come from, see my friend snatching them up in her flurried run from front door to gate, with the grass plucked from the clump beside the tree on the nature strip as she scrambled into the car. And then, after all her flurry, I had been sleeping.

The bouquet kept me company for the rest of the afternoon. Especially the lantana. I had forgotten about lantana, and what these commonplace, marvellous flowers once meant, what they still mean, to me.

In those days, in the early forties, neighbours didn't go into each other's houses, or not in our street. Kids were the messengers—

preferably kids under ten. I suppose the grown-ups thought we wouldn't notice too much. We'd fly like skinny pigeons between the back doors with notes asking for half a cup of Rinso until Friday or whatever. So when Mum decided to buy her eggs from the Wans down the hill—they kept chooks in their backyard—I was the one who went to fetch them. The Wans were our local gentry. People used to say they'd come down in the world. I imagined the three of them peering over the edge of the basket of a hot-air balloon, bumping down in their front garden. When I asked my mother, she said they'd been 'big people in the country', which didn't make much sense either. But I could see they were different from everybody else, because they never borrowed anything or talked over the side fence, and they never went to the shops. They had everything delivered.

So twice a week I'd open the latch on the curly iron gate that was a bit off its hinges, edge through, click it shut, go down the narrow side path and past the lattice and around to the kitchen, tap on the flywire door, and when it opened hold out my note. The eldest sister, the one I called the boss Miss Wan, was always the one who came. She ran the house and looked after the egg money and the grocery order and things like that. She was as long and bony and yellow as a skeleton, and she always dressed in black, and at first I was scared of her.

The one I called the middle Miss Wan might really have been the youngest—there were still some red streaks in the grey hair sticking out under the squashed brown hat she always wore, and she was sort of gangly, the way some girls are—but because the third sister was tiny and round and pretty in a dim sort of way, she was the one I called the baby Miss Wan. The baby Miss Wan looked after the vegetable garden and the fruit trees. Sometimes she'd sneak a furry biscuit or an apple as wrinkled as her cheeks into my hand, as if she didn't want the boss Miss Wan to see, but she wasn't really worried. She just enjoyed secrets. Whenever they were together all three of them would be suddenly gay, pleased with each other, like girls at a party, and the baby Miss Wan was always the merriest of the lot.

It was the middle Miss Wan I liked best. I suppose she was what they used to call 'a bit slow'. Thinking back, I'm not even sure she could talk. I can't remember her ever saying anything. She'd tell me what to do with tugs and pats of her big red hands, and jerk her chin when she wanted me to look at something, with her big old eyes so bright that you had to look, and it would be a spider web covered in dew or something like that. Everything made her happy. She'd tug me into the chook yard, give a few high clucks in her throat, and her pet bantams and the big Rhode Island Reds would come rushing up, squawking and squabbling over the handful of wheat she'd give me to scatter. If I was there early enough she'd let me mix the morning bran mash—it smelt better than any porridge—and scoop it into the feeding trough, and she'd guide my hand into the laying boxes, right in under the shifting feathers, and I'd touch something sleek and warm and lift out the heavy egg, and she'd smile right into my eyes like a baby.

Grown-ups would often try to pump me about the Wans. I didn't tell them anything, partly because I liked being the only one to know what went on behind the high fence, but mostly because it was so different from everything outside the gate that I didn't know how to describe it. It was wholly different place in there. I don't think the grown-ups minded. They liked the Wans to be mysterious. To begin with Mum was nervous about my visiting them at all. She was always coaching me about 'manners', and in one of her grabs at being a lady she tried to get me to call them 'the Misses Wan' instead of just 'the Miss Wans', saying it showed more respect. At first she was shocked by the names I'd given them, but she fetched up using them herself, because how else could we tell them apart?

After a while the boss Miss Wan started asking me into the kitchen. It was scrubbed, bare—nothing like the kitchen at home. Then she'd take me by the shoulders with her thin cold hands and stand me at the entrance to the dining room, so I could admire it, with its long mahogany table and the chairs standing around, and the dark sideboard with the metal pheasant on it, everything shining and smelling of polish, and not a sign of food or eating anywhere. Once she led me over to the sideboard and slid out one of the drawers, so I could see what was inside: glossy white tablecloths—best damask, she said—and giant napkins with sharp creases, all beautifully folded away. And then the cutlery drawer. We only had the knife drawer at home, with everything tossed in higgledy-piggledy, but in Miss Wan's drawer there were four of each kind of thing—four sorts of knives, four sorts of forks and spoons, then ladles, carving forks, a carving knife nearly as big as a sword—and every single one of them made out of heavy silver and laid out in satin-lined boxes like little padded coffins, so that they took up the whole length of the long drawer. And even in the darkness I could see that the round glass lamps along the sideboard shone like rubies hung with ice-crystal stars. It was then I got to like the boss Miss Wan, because she touched these things so tenderly, not because she was proud to own them, but because they were beautiful.

All three walls were covered in photographs: old, brown ones, in heavy frames. It was always dim in there, like being underwater, with the blinds pulled down even in winter, and fine net curtains on top of them, and dark green velvet drapes at the sides, but after a while your eyes got used to it. There was one picture I especially liked, of a handsome young man, in profile, with a stiff collar up to his chin and a lot of dark hair rippling back from his forehead. It hung exactly above the centre of the sideboard. When Miss Wan saw me looking at it she nodded to the picture, and said something strange. She said: 'He is our only brother. He fell in Flanders field.' She should have said *was* our brother.

Over the mantelpiece, behind the chair at the head of the table, was the biggest picture of the lot, in a heavy oval frame. It was a 'studio portrait' of the father, Mr Wan. He looked ferocious, like men did in the old days, with a thin tight mouth in a great bush of whiskers, and squinty angry eyes glaring down on the room and everyone in it. I thought he might have been a missionary, because there was another photograph of him looking huge and angry in front of some little Chinese boys, very neat and clean, sitting with their white-socked feet crossed and their blank faces looking straight at the camera.

Opposite Mr Wan, in her own smaller frame, just above what must have been her chair when she was alive, was a hand-coloured picture of the mother. She had darkish hair, perhaps red, like the stuff that sprouted from under the middle Miss Wan's hat, and she had the round cheeks and the vague prettiness of the baby Miss Wan. The boss Miss Wan looked more like her father—thin mouth, pale eyes—but sadder, and nothing like as angry.

I'm not sure if Mr Wan really was a missionary—I might have thought that just because of the face, and the photograph, and that funny name, 'Wan'. And because of what happened next, because the Miss Wans, or more likely the boss Miss Wan, decided to do something about my religious education.

It's true I hadn't had any, except for learning a bit about mission-aries in religious instruction at school. My mother said that religion was good for children, but she'd never got around to doing anything about it. I don't know how Miss Wan arranged it. Did she give me a note for my mother? I can't imagine her coming out of her gate, walking up the hill, turning in at our gate, climbing our scruffy steps, knocking on our door. She never went into the street—only the baby Miss Wan, sometimes, with her grey felt hat pulled down to her nose and in a great hurry—so it must have been a note. I do know that one Sunday morning my mother scrubbed and dressed me, tonged my hair into bends, gave me a shilling for 'the collection' and told me to go down to the Misses Wan and to do everything they told me.

They took me to the big stone church in Noble Street. I expect-ed to enjoy myself, and I did. I loved the singing, the way the boys' voices floated around the vaulted ceiling, the flowers in their tall brass urns, the sweet, stifling smell of the smoke coming out of the golden balls, the sun setting fire to the stained-glass windows, and best of all the processions of solemn men, with their high hats, their robes, their embroidered stoles. I'd had no idea that such things went on inside those old grey buildings. I imitated everything the Miss Wans did, though when I went to follow the boss Miss Wan up to the front where people were kneeling in a row, the baby Miss Wan gently pulled me back, so I waited in the pew until all three had gone up and taken bird-sips from the silver jug and opened their mouths wide for the priest.

This going to church happened quite often for a while. Perhaps they took me whenever they went themselves. I don't think they were regular churchgoers. They were too shy for that, and no-one ever spoke to them. Perhaps they went because they didn't want me to grow up a heathen—the baby Miss Wan used to sing a song about saving the heathen. I think they liked going to church because it was so rich and vivid compared to their quiet underwater lives. I liked it because it was so orderly and peaceful. At home it was always noisy, with the six of us piled into one small house. When my father came home at night we'd all be in the kitchen, with the radio on and homework spread out and the dinner cooking, and he'd stamp in saying, 'It's the Human Zoo and HERE COMES THE KEEPER', though really we managed pretty well, threading round each other on our own little tracks.

The Wans never talked to me about what happened inside the church. I suppose they hoped some of it would just rub off, though it never did. The funny thing is that in spite of all that religion I committed my first and only sin because of the Wans. My mother always taught us that stealing was the worst thing you could do— she would have approved of the Muslims chopping off people's hands for stealing the smallest thing, like an apple or an old crust of bread. But there was a bush with dull green sticky leaves that grew halfway down the Wan's side path, and it was covered with the most beautiful flowers I had ever seen. They were very small, and they were like fairy bouquets, with different coloured flowers—pink, pale yellow, lavender—arranged in perfect circles. It was lantana, I discovered later, and it grows like a weed further north. I was too shy to stop and look at one properly, and I couldn't ask (my mother thought asking for things, even accepting things when they were offered, was almost as bad as stealing) but I desperately wanted one.

So I decided to steal one. I planned it: if I wore my apron with the big front pocket I could snatch a flower head on the way past, hide it in my pocket, and then when I got home I could crawl under the house and duck-waddle through the dry powdery dust to the furthest corner, which was my own place for being private. (I was the smallest, so no-one else could get in so far.) And then I would look at the bouquet-flower for as long as I wanted.

I wasn't scared of the Miss Wans: I knew they wouldn't mind, not even the boss Miss Wan. It was God I was worried about. The first time I tried, with my heart thumping and my stomach shaking and His great mad eye glaring full at me like Mr Wan's, I couldn't do it. But the next time I did it almost without thinking—my hand just floated out, nipped off a flower, it was in my pocket, I was out the gate and home free. In the dusty golden light under the house it was as beautiful as I thought it would be. And nothing happened. My hand didn't wither, nobody found out, nothing bad happened at all. That's when I found out what I'd always suspected, that God was a fraud. So that was the end of Him, and of sin.

I longed to see more of the Wan house: the bedrooms, and especially the bathroom, because bathrooms are always interesting. Once I'd got into Mrs Mack's, the uphill neighbour, by saying I needed to use the lavatory. Her bathroom was all pink and smelling of powder, with her pink shower cap hanging on a little hook and a pink cosy on the lavatory seat, and no trace of Mr Mack anywhere. I wouldn't have dared try that with the boss Miss Wan, but one day when I was in the chook yard with the middle Miss Wan I whispered that I needed to go. She looked flustered for a moment, so I was sorry I'd asked, but then she led me to a broken-down outside lavatory beside the little toolshed, bowed me in, and showed me how she'd stand guard at the door, banging her old rake down between her feet and standing to attention like a soldier. She was always making jokes like that, and making me laugh.

That must have been the lavatory she and her sister used, at least in the daytime. While they did a lot of their work outside, in what I suppose used to be the country way when they were girls—peeling and slicing the fruit they were putting up for the winter in the garden shed, stacking the jars along the shelves, burying lemons in sawdust, rubbing eggs with isinglass so they'd keep—they must have had a room somewhere inside the house for cooking and eating and ironing and talking, and for when the weather was bad. The war with Germany and Japan was still happening then, but it wasn't happening at the Wan house. They didn't even have a radio, and if they ever mentioned the war they meant the first one against Germany, the one with their brother in it. When I was in bed I liked to think of the sisters all snug together inside their house down the hill, girlish and gay, sewing, drawing maps, doing sums, learning poetry—the kinds of things girls did in the old books I read.

I never knew if my imagined inside room existed. I never saw past the dining room. No-one else saw inside the house at all. If a delivery man came to the front door, the boss Miss Wan would unlock the door and open it just a crack, and tell them to go around the back, and she'd meet them at the kitchen door, and call the baby Miss Wan to take the box inside. (No-one else locked their doors in our street—we didn't even have a key to our house.)

It's only now I realise that in spite of all that expensive household stuff they didn't have any money. The musty biscuits, the raggy clothes and the sacking aprons of the two younger ones, the lack of food-smells in the kitchen, the cold inside even in mid-winter, should have told me that, but to me they were just marks of their aristocratic ways.

Then things began to go wrong at the Wans. The boss Miss Wan suddenly seemed to get much older. When I'd call for the eggs she'd be slow coming to the door, and she'd peer at me a bit uncertainly, as if she didn't quite know who I was. And the front of her dress would sometimes be buttoned up in the wrong holes, or have some food dribbled down it, or its white collar would be on a bit crooked—just little things, but shocking to see in her. And the baby Miss Wan began leaving whatever she was doing in the garden and coming into the house with me, though it was still the boss Miss Wan who gave me the eggs and took the money.

Then one hot afternoon the baby Miss Wan must have been busy, and didn't hear me arrive. I tapped on the door, and at last the boss Miss Wan came wavering from somewhere deep inside, and slowly led me into the kitchen. A blowfly was blundering against the corner of the kitchen window. Miss Wan looked at it, then shot out her hand, grabbed it in her fingertips, and squeezed it—I can still hear the fly's buzzing change pitch—until the yellow insides squirted out over her pale skin. Then she dropped the emptied body, looked down at her fingers, bent her head down like an animal, and licked them clean. The baby Miss Wan had just come in. We looked at each other, I picked up the eggs, thanked her, and managed to get out of the house before I started to heave.

I think I saw the Wan sisters, at least to talk to, only once after that. Again it was hot, again the eldest Miss Wan came slowly out of the darkness, peering at me out of her strained old eyes. Big tears began to leak out of them, making little rivulets along the fine wrinkles until they collected in the corners of her mouth, and her long pale tongue came out and mumbled the tears up as she looked at me, so sad, so sad. I put my hand out to her, and she took hold of it and then of my arm, and began to stroke the skin, murmuring, 'Such a lovely blouse—like silk, like silk,' with the big tears falling. I could smell her smell, something sour under the lavender water.

Then her sister put her arm around her waist, and led her away.

I let myself out. The middle Miss Wan, standing in the yard, gave me a little salute as I turned down the side path. I knew I wouldn't be visiting them again. They'd have to close ranks now. There would be no room for outsiders.

I crawled under the house for a while, to be sure of being on my own, and then went inside, gave my mother the eggs, and told her the Wans didn't want to sell eggs any more, that they were getting rid of the chooks. She must have seen I'd been crying, and asked me if I was all right, but when I said I was fine she didn't ask any questions. She just nodded.

I've never told anyone about those last visits, but somehow the neighbourhood knew that something was happening. It was public soon enough anyway, because the boss Miss Wan began to escape. We'd see her, skinny legs pumping, black skirts flapping, racing up the hill, full of a terrible energy. The strength might have left her mind, but her body was frighteningly tough. After her would come the baby Miss Wan, apple cheeks flaming, to catch her arm and coax until she'd turn for home. But sometimes she wouldn't turn, and the baby Miss Wan couldn't hold her, so the middle Miss Wan would have to help, rushing stiff-legged and awkward, boots clumping, wild hair flying under her hat. Watching from behind the bedroom curtain I would think of her hens, rushing towards her, stiff-legged and awkward. Frantic. Then they'd catch the boss Miss Wan and pull her wailing down the street, wailing through the curly white gate, wailing down the narrow path past the lantana bush.

At first my mother would send me down to the sealed house with an apple pie or some of her potted steak, and I'd add them to the offerings lined up on the doorstep in front of the closed back door. Ants were swarming all over them. The door would not be opened again. Not to us.

Not to anyone else, either. Different people—men from the council, the district nurse, once two young policemen—came and beat on their front door, but no-one answered. They'd go down the side, then after a while they'd come out again and ask along the street for information, but no-one knew anything. They came to our house a couple of times. My mother, usually so timid with strangers and always so stern about lying, would look them in the eye and say no, she hadn't seen anything of the old ladies, perhaps they were away visiting, no, she couldn't say where, no, she hadn't noticed anything out of the ordinary, as far as she knew they were perfectly well, no, she couldn't be any help at all. I'd never known her so steely.

When the bad time began a few people tried to start stories about cruelties in the Wan household, about starvation and beatings and cords cutting into old flesh. You know the kind of thing. You know the kind of people. The neighbourhood would have none of it, and froze them into silence. The street, usually fat with gossip, knew when it was time to turn its face away, that the sisters had chosen, that they would manage, or not manage, on their own.

I don't remember when they died, or anything of funerals or hearses or the busywork of death. Did a nephew come? I don't remember. They had chosen to cease to exist for us long before they died.

This was meant to be a story of the Wan sisters, but it isn't a story because in a way nothing happened to them, nothing at all. All around them things, people, the world changed. They didn't. They went on living as their father had told them to live all those years ago, dancing the ghostly dances of girlhood in that bleak house, their refuge, their temple, their prison, their palace.

The house is still there. A young family lives in it now, but it looks much the same, though the lantana has gone, and there are toys on the grass where the baby Miss Wan, blushing in the heat of the public gaze, used to push her rattly lawn-mower every fine Thursday. It's still called 'the Wan house', even by people who arrived in the street long after the sisters were gone. The young couple say, 'We live in the Wan house', with a pleased air of distinction. I used to pass it often when my parents were alive, and every time I would think of them: the boss Miss Wan, preserving in her own fastidious person a family's ferocious pride. The baby Miss Wan with her wrinkles and dimples and her pretty-girl ways, still winsome at eighty. And the middle Miss Wan in her squashed clown's hat, happy among her hens, never knowing that the world might see her as a figure of fun, protected as much by her simplicity as by the tough, abiding love of her sisters.

It was an honour to have known them, the Misses Wan.

THE YEAR OF THE FOREIGN DOCTOR

I had incited memory in my hospital bed. Now it roared like angry bees.

I was nine or ten when the Wans closed their doors against the street. I was about twelve when my mother arranged for me to spend the summer holidays with her youngest sister and her children at Wye River, a beach and a hill with a scatter of cottages about twenty kilometres beyond Lorne. It was hot every day that summer, with the war over at last. If it rained at all it rained at night, hammering on the tin roof, clucking into the tank. The house had been put together, thrown together my father said, by a family who had run away from the misery of life in Geelong during the Depression, and they'd used anything and everything they could lay their hands on—sleepers, old weatherboards, bricks, corrugated iron, anything to keep out the wind and the rain. And it had turned out beautifully. They could have built anywhere seeing they were just borrowing the land— down in the valley, on the side of the hill closest to the sea—but instead they'd chosen the most difficult site, I think because they wanted the view in both directions. They'd run the house right along the spine of the ridge, so the three rooms were all long and thin: the one for cooking and eating in the middle and a thinner one on each side, and a midget bathroom opening off the kitchen leaning against the back. They'd tacked on a louvred verandah at the front for sitting around during the summer. You could imagine them all squeezed around the narrow table in the middle room with their hurricane lamp and the stove keeping them warm, eating rabbits and fish and crays and fruit pies and congratulating themselves on getting away from the sadness and the bread-and-dripping sixty or seventy kilo- metres away in Geelong.

By the time my aunt started renting the place for the summers the people were long gone and the house was looking frail and worn, but enduring in the way old home-built houses and some old people do. The verandah had begun to sag, but inside every joint was snug and it still stood squarely on its little wooden stumps, except for the lean-to at the back, which was close to collapsing. The water had to be heated in kettles on the stove, so we only used the old bath for bucket-baths if it was too cold to swim, and to drown the crayfish we caught, dry claws scrabbling on the mottled tin. We stacked the rest of the lean-to with firewood, and kept the fishing gear in there.

My aunt's husband had died when her children were very young. She resisted unhappiness by looking after everybody else, and she always took a tribe of children with her to the beach house. Both the skinny side-rooms (boys on one side, girls on the other) were crammed edge to edge with old double beds, like New Guinean sleeping platforms. We would all go to bed at the same time, and crawl to our particular spot, and when the last one was in my aunt would douse the hurricane lamp and get into the bed she'd make up on the sofa on the verandah, and she'd leave the torch on the floor beside her in case any of us had to get up in the night. I always had to. They must have built the outhouse last, when they'd really got the hang of it, because it was beautiful—very exact, with every one of its silvery boards fitting trim and neat. Years later, when I saw the delicate wooden buildings in Shaker territory in Pennsylvania, I remembered the outhouse at Wye.

To get to it you had to negotiate the muscly white roots of the big gum, duck under the fence—the people who built the house had proudly marked off their illegal territory with a single strand of knee-high wire—and go up a notional track. Further down the ridge there were the remains of old gardens—geraniums, moth-eaten irises, whole jungles of ochre nasturtiums and their frail green leaves as thin and clinging as human skin—but up by the outhouse the bush was dry and scruffy, with lots of bracken and blackberry and the trees small and tired-looking. Every year I'd begin by being shocked at how ugly it was, and then a couple of hours later I'd be thinking it was very pretty. Inside the outhouse was good too, with the wooden bench smooth and warm on your bottom, the sharp smell of Phenol, the neat squares of newspaper on the wire spike, and in the afternoons the blowflies drowsing high on the wall. No spiders either, or none I ever saw. There wasn't a dunny man, not in those days, so the boy cousins used to empty the can, but one week they were off on a camp and my aunt said it was a crisis so I did it. It turned out to be simple, chip-chipping away with the mattock at the bony ground until I had a decent-sized hole, dragging the can over, tipping the stuff in, burying it—it was just a brown sludge, smelling of Phenol if anything, and when I came back to the house my aunt said I was a hero. But she backed away as she said it.

I liked the outhouse best on moonlit nights, because then the moonlight would come slicing through the slim black gumleaves like hard silver rain. Over a few of those nights I made friends with a feral kitten who lived under the floor. There were other kittens under there, I could hear them, but they wouldn't come out. She did, but not far, for the meat scraps I would bring her. She wouldn't let me touch her, but after she had eaten she would crouch, tuck in her paws, wrap her rat-tail around her, lift her chin, and make a weird high thin humming, more a song than a purr, as her pale round eyes gathered the moonlight in.

The boys' sleepout looked over to the sea: to the headland, the beach where we swam, and over the empty ocean. On our side the blond flanks of the hill rippled down to the spread of the valley, with the dairy sheds huddled against the wall of the mountains and the cleft of the river at the far end, and Mr Wilmott's milkers dotted around like animals from a Noah's Ark. The whole end wall of our sleepout was bookshelves, stuffed with the overflow from I don't know whose houses, and late in the afternoons when we had come in and my aunt was cooking the dinner we'd read on our beds, with the sun pouring in, and voices from the valley and the crooning of the cows mixed in with the sounds of the sea. I'd read every single one of those books every year, especially the Conan Doyles. Each afternoon Baker Street fog and the smoke from Holmes's pipe would hang in the clear Australian air.

Ben lived further down the ridge in a renovated cottage. He was three years older than I was, which is a lot when you're twelve, and he was the most sensible and skilful person I had ever met: he could tickle trout, shoot rabbits, set craypots, catch fish off the rocks, every-thing. He didn't mind if I tagged along provided I made myself useful, so when the others headed off to the beach with the cricket bat and the inner tube we'd go up the river or rock-fishing, or generally scout around.

Going up the river took a lot of gear: the big water bottle, the gun, the fish-spear, the bag and my haversack with the lunches. Ben would take the gun and sling the empty bag over his shoulder and tie it fore and aft to his belt, and I'd trot along behind him with the rest like a squaw. Which made sense: you can't be too careful carrying a gun, and I liked him going ahead anyway, because of the snakes. You didn't see many when you were moving, but you could hear them, rustling away through the dry leaves.

It was a beautiful river, small—four hours would see you to the source—but with all the joys of a big one: soprano rapids, tenor waterfalls, baritone backwaters with water-boatmen clog-dancing and gumleaves waltzing. I'd heard no Mozart then, but now I think of it as a Mozartian river, it was so confident and shapely.

I think my father felt much the same way. 'Better than anything in Europe,' he'd say, waving at the waterlilies and the native violets and the tumbled rocks, which were everything from granite to ochre or black honeycomb—my father, who had seen only one torn corner of France, who came to the beach house only once, who had never got further up river than the first big pool, but who could always find good words for what he was looking at.

When Ben and I had a day up the river we'd make our last stop at the big pool on the way home to wrap the trout in bracken and pack them into my haversack, empty now the lunches were eaten. He'd tell me to wait fifteen minutes or so, and he would head off across the valley with the eels and the rabbits and the legal stuff in his bag (he had a licence for the twenty-two) in case the Fisheries and Wildlife men stopped him, because they stopped him every single time they saw him. They knew he was taking trout all right. What they could never figure out was how he was getting them home.

They stopped me just once, in my third summer there. They asked me what the eel spear was for. It was just a sawn-off broom handle with three big iron barbs bound on the end, but it could come in handy working the deeper pools. Yes, we did use it on trout sometimes, but only when we'd located one exactly and couldn't get it any other way. I was afraid that if I opened my mouth they'd see my heart beating—it felt as if it had come right up into my throat—but I managed to say my big brother had made it for me so snakes wouldn't bother me, and they laughed and said the snakes had better watch out, and the tall one with the narrow teeth said we were old friends already because he watched me every morning cutting across the valley to the dairy with the billies to get the milk for my auntie, and I stood there grinning and sweating and smelling the trout even through the bracken, and when they'd joked and grinned long enough, they let me go. It was just as well they expected fourteen-year-old girls to be idiots. When I finally got up to the stand of bluegums where Ben was waiting he was still white.

I'd seen the Fisheries and Wildlife men before, although they didn't know it. One day we left the eel spear and the bag with some trout, including a huge one Ben had been after for weeks, on the sandy backflow of a pool, and went upriver to get some rabbits for dinner. We were well up onto the plateau when we heard them. They had been fishing, and now they were heading downstream, talking, but moving very fast. Even in my panic I had to admire how neat-footed they were over the rocks. We both knew I would have to be the one to try to beat them back to our stuff, because if they got even a glimpse of Ben they'd be after him.

I was smaller, almost as fast, and being a girl a lot less suspicious, although what I was meant to say if they caught me haring through the bush I could not imagine. I'd taken off a sandal to check a blister, but I didn't dare stop to put it on; I was off and running as hard as I've ever run, blood huffing in my ears, the elephant grass and the occasional blackberry slashing my face, and whispering 'no snakes no snakes please no snakes' as I ran. After what felt like an hour (it can't have been more than five minutes) there was the little beach and the spear and the bag.

I grabbed them and splashed across the river and up the far bank, backed deep into a boobialla bush and pulled them in after me. Then I squatted down and tried to get my breath back.

For the longest time nothing happened. I began to feel like an idiot, squatting in my little green burrow, and I was thinking about coming out. And then, suddenly, there they were, framed in the boobialla. They'd passed the higher pools because they'd been waiting for this one. They took a couple of minutes to organise their rods, very dedicated and solemn, and then they began flicking the lines out over the water. The tall one with the long teeth had a magic wrist: he'd float the line out like gossamer, and drop it just where he wanted. He must have been after the big one Ben had taken that morning, because he worked the pool for quite a while, until at last the other man made him pack up and move on. I could have told them they were wasting their time. There'd be no fish in that pool for a month. Trout put a sign up when there have been ticklers around.

When they'd gone Ben eased out of the bushes on the other side, and we went home. I don't know why, but I remember that as one of the best times of my life, after all the running and panic, crouching there while the men were fishing, and neither of them knowing that I was in the boobialla, watching.

It was around about the time the Fisheries and Wildlife men stopped me that the big grey car turned up in Cartridge Valley. Most of those places didn't have names. We called it that because once we found a lot of spent cartridges there. Usually there was nothing, just the creek and the reeds and sometimes a stray heifer from Wilmott's farm chewing the soft grass on the little flat. This time there was the car, and a man and a woman trying to put up a shabby old tent with not the faintest notion how to do it. We were watching from the hill when the man spotted us and waved, so we had to go down.

I didn't like the look of them. They were foreigners, for one thing. The woman was bone-thin, with wisps of pale frayed-looking hair sticking out from a scarf wound tight as a bandage around her head. I still don't know if she spoke any English: she just stood at the man's shoulder and nodded and smiled and made little murmurs. He talked enough for both of them, very fast and saying some of the words wrong, but after a while you got used to it. He was short, with a wrinkled monkey face and a long coat draggling to his ankles, even though I could see the sweat shining on his forehead. I remember thinking he looked like a slater, all long grey coat and nervous little feet and the little head poking out the top wincing in the sunlight.

The moment we got the tent up he started asking questions. Where did we live, did we have parents, did we like school, how many brothers and sisters, what were their names—silly questions, who didn't have parents, who didn't go to school, but he went on and on, urgently, as if the answers mattered. Avid, somehow. I hated it, so like the wife I stood behind Ben, staring at my feet and wishing he'd shut up so we could get away.

Ben didn't seem to mind. For one thing he was used to foreigners; in fact his own mother was foreign, French or Belgian or something. His father had brought her back from the war, my father's war, the Great War, and then he had died. I'd only seen her once, when Ben sent me back to fetch a knife he wanted. She never seemed to come out of the house. It was dim inside, with every curtain drawn, and although the house was small the rooms seemed to flow away forever. She was dim too, a soft, floury woman in a dark silky dress with small black eyes and a small weak voice and round pencilled-in black eyebrows. For a while I wondered how someone like Ben could have come out of that house, and out of that woman. Then I forgot about it.

Ben stood, relaxed and easy, answering the questions, but I could tell he was getting fed up, and when the man asked the names of the schools we went to when we weren't on holidays, Ben said, still easy and friendly, 'Why? Why do you want to know?'

The man flinched as if he had been hit, and his face crumpled— for a moment I thought he was going to cry—and the woman's hand flew up and tugged at those straggly bits of hair. Then she scurried over to the car, dragged the boot open and fossicked out a big red and gold biscuit tin. They were not like any biscuits I'd ever seen, not Date Bars or Choco-Malts or anything like that, but big as cakes, and the thick chocolate coatings had melted and stuck together in the heat. She kept jerking the tin at our faces, and she seemed upset so we each prised one out, and then kept grinning and waving them about and saying yes, yes, they were delicious.

When we'd licked our fingers more or less clean Ben asked a question. Was that blood on the inside of the car? When I looked I saw it too: long rusty smears all over the back windows. The man brightened and said, yes, it was snake's blood. His wife put a hand on his shoulder and whispered something, but he just stroked the hand and went on. He was conducting an experiment, a very important experiment about snake venom he'd begun a long time ago, when he'd had a proper laboratory, with assistants and all the snakes he needed. He hesitated, looking sort of puzzled, and the wife whispered to him again, and then he got back on track and said how difficult it was now: he was trying to continue his work but he hardly ever got hold of a snake, and when he did and he'd milked the venom he didn't have anywhere to keep it. So then he would kill it in the car, for safety.

It sounded weird to me. I'd never heard of anyone doing experiments on snakes, and there were no cages or anything like that around, just ordinary camp muddle. And why kill them? Why not just let them go? But Ben was listening very seriously, and nodding, so perhaps it made sense. Then the man asked us if we happened to know anything about snakes. We told him there were a lot of tigers and copperheads around but hardly any browns, and he asked us if we could catch some for him, he didn't care what kind, and he'd give us two, no, five shillings apiece for them. And we could call him Doctor, and his wife Madame Lise.

Five shillings was a lot of money in those days, just after the war, so we tried it. It was hard work, more hot and annoying than dangerous once you knew how to work the noose and the stick, and in the first week we caught four. They were only little ones, the biggest not much over half a metre, but the Doctor paid us just the same. I'd begun to like him because he'd get so excited when we brought him his weary little snakes. Madame Lise didn't change, though—she'd stand behind him, smiling, with her eyes slithering around. Then I thought she was frightened of him. Now I think she was frightened of us.

A couple of weeks later everything was wrecked. The Doctor had given me the head of one of the copperheads mounted on a pretty pale blue saucer, propped so you could look right into the creamy mouth with the delicate white fangs curving down. I couldn't risk putting it in my haversack in case it broke, so I tried to smuggle it into the house under my shirt. My aunt saw it, and the whole story came out. She didn't say anything, but the next morning the local constable just happened to drop by the camp, and when we got there late in the afternoon they were gone. They'd left some rubbish—they didn't know a thing about camping—so we buried it, and mooned around for a while, wondering where they'd gone and whether it was worth trying to find them. Then we went home.

So that was the end of the Doctor. It was really the end of the beach house, too, and of a lot of other things. The next year Ben went to the university, and brought a girl back who only wanted to lie around on the beach all summer, so we didn't go up the river any more, and a few weeks later I got into a bit of trouble one night at the local camping ground. The man didn't know I was under sixteen, and I didn't know that it mattered. My aunt came looking for me some time after midnight and found me in his car. She didn't say much—I don't think she even told my mother—but she sent me home early, and she didn't ask me to stay again after that.

I didn't care. It was a good house and a good place, and I was as happy there as I ever have been. But it was finished. Years later friends told me they were going to give me a surprise and took me there on our way to somewhere else. There were houses all over the hillside and spilling down into the valley, shrinking everything, flattening all the shapes. The river track had gone altogether, vanished under a blanket of blackberry, and a 'local' told me there had never been a track. The rocky track we used to climb from the beach, thighs aching, had turned into a sealed road; the car swept up it in less than a minute. All the shacks along the ridge were gone, along with the irises and the geraniums and the nasturtiums, and a brown brick villa squatted on a scrubby little lawn where our place used to be. No trace of the gum. They must have had a bobcat in because even the roots were gone. I couldn't recognise anything.

But the bush above was still too steep to build on, so I skirted the fence and found a way up. There was a flood of rubbish down the side gully—those so-neat people in the neat little villa had been dumping it there—and nearby a few silvery, splintery boards were sticking out of the scrabble of bracken. The outhouse, or what was left of it.

I don't think about the beach house now, or the people I knew there. You think it was Ben bringing his girl that ended it, that I was jealous, adolescent, couldn't handle it? I heard you counting: 'Fifteen!' That wasn't it. I didn't have a crush on Ben. I didn't want to touch him, I didn't want him to touch me. I just loved him: loved his steady walk and his clear brown skin, his solid good temper, his competence. The man in the car was about being fifteen. I'd seen him one day on the beach, and the next night at a dance at a tiny logging place down the coast I'd gone to with my cousin and his girlfriend. He was from the city, and older than most of the people there, twenty-five maybe, and his shirt was very white, so white you could see the blue shadows in it, and his face and hands very dark. From the moment I saw the glimmer of his shirt and his dark face on the other side of the dusty hall I couldn't see anything else. Then he came over, threading sleekly through the dancers and asked me to dance, and I saw the white shirt and the dark face very close, and then he took my hand in his dark one and I felt the warmth of his other hand on the small of my back and I could smell the warm clean smell of cotton and under that the salty tang of his skin, and my buttocks clenched and my face flamed and great quivering vibrations started radiating out from his hand and zinging down my legs and making my thighs shake so that I couldn't move my legs, but could only lean against him. That was being fifteen.

It was the foreign doctor and his wife who ended it, because they taught me that my sunlit valley was not to be confused with the world. They still visit me sometimes, uninvited, always welcome. I will be sleeping and suddenly there they are, standing in their messy camp in the sun-struck valley, waving, just as they used to when they saw us coming down the shadowed hill, but urgently, silently, like dead people in a dream. They seem to be signalling to me. They must be long dead by now, but I still think about them. I still worry about them: where did they go when they were driven out of the valley? Where could they go, running from their past? Because now I know where they had come from, what they were running from. Now I know why she kept those biscuits melting in their beautiful red and gold tin, she who held to life only because of her terrified, despairing love for her husband. And the Doctor, with his loving little gifts, his dream-talk of laboratories and experiments, his wistful fascination with the sweet ordinariness of the lives of two ordinary kids. What did he think about, what faces did he see as he beat the innocent little snakes in the old grey car? Whose blood was it splattering on the glass?

TRANSITIONS

Eel or Trout?

Writing my childhood has made me see that the marshland between memory and invention is treacherous. I did not know how the Wan sisters filled most of their days and all of their nights, because I saw them only in daylight glimpses, but as a child I deeply enjoyed imagining what they might have done when I was not there to see. As for the accuracy of actual memories, now I have written them down—there really was a house between the sea and a river, a boy and an aunt, a foreign doctor and a wife. The biscuits and the snakes were real. It is the girl I have most doubts about. But there she is, on the page. She looks real enough there.

It is only now, half a century after the events I have been describing, that I realise the Olympian authority of writing. Before I began to retrieve my five-year-old Herbie-worshipping self, my eight-year-old egg-buying self and those unreliable adolescent selves from beach-house summers, they had been lying around inside my head like a clutter of old photographs in a forgotten drawer. Now they have been pulled out and arranged in an ordered sequence of pages, a material bundle existing within the material world. They have also moved decisively from hidden through private to public. They are now open to your inspection.

There has been another, subtler translation. Now that they are fixed, existing as things in this world, there is no-one but me to say how true they are, and no-one but me to care.

And, of course, I do care. Historians live by believing truth can be extracted from people's memories, including their written memories. Yet when I read my memories I am uneasy. I do not recognise the girl's temperament as continuous with mine. I don't think I was ever so competent. I think her competence might be an artefact of the writing. But it is also true that when I pulled her out from the rubble of time I discovered something about myself I had not known before. I escaped the Fisheries and Wildlife men that long-ago day, still clear as glass in memory, but my illegal trout tickling had consequences.

Tickling trout is an addictive enterprise. You find a likely river, a likely pool and, placing yourself in knee- to hip-deep water, you begin feeling delicately along banks, under rock ledges, around the edges of boulders. You map in your mind the underwater topography—here weeds, here gravel, here a shelving fall.

And then, if you are lucky, your fingertips touch something, a living something, holding against the current and very slightly vibrating. Your job is to move your fingers tenderly along its length. Now you are mapping the body of the fish—praying it will curve and swell, that it is not long and thin and sinisterly muscled, that it will not transform under your fingers into a vicious-toothed eel—until you have exactly learnt it with your blind fingertips: here the tail, here the head, here and here the gills. And all the while tenderly, tenderly stroking, so that the fish is mesmerised by the sliding fingers.

The end is brutal: thumb and index finger driven hard into the gills, a full-arm backwards toss, and a radiant trout is flapping in the grass, losing colour as you look at it.

Taking the trout, cooking and eating the trout, matter, but it is that moment of tactile encounter which is supreme—the blind exploration, the tentative construction of an actual but concealed creature, of an actual but concealed world, from a series of obscure intimations. I think I developed a taste for ethnographic history tickling trout in the Wye River. The moment of touching the trout, when you know you touch some quite different way of being in the world, some previously inaccessible creature, as you gently, gently test to see if the shape is indeed as you think it might be— that is also the supreme moment, the surpassing magic, of doing history.

Is truth an eel? Or a trout?

Hospitals respect neither moods nor memories. They are the Now, and impose their own rigorous, obscure, testing agendas.

A woman was brought into the ward last night about an hour after lights out. There was no bed for her, so they closed our curtains and parked her trolley between the rows. She was confused but conscious: she must have thought she was in a tunnel made of pale blue sheets, with an oblong of light at the end. A resident was with her. I think he gave her an injection. He must have been doing something, because she kept thanking him, and apologising for being a nuisance. He said, 'That's all right.' Not a word more. Listening, I wanted to slice him into pieces.

He went away, and there was silence for a while. I heard her crying, very softly, and then a breathy whisper, like a five-year-old put to bed and told to be quiet, 'Nurse?' And crying again.

My bell was pinned to my sheet, so I rang it. The nurse padded in, looked, went out, and I heard the ping of the telephone. He spoke to someone, then dialled again and asked for Dr Someone in Intensive Care, murmured for a moment and hung up.

Almost immediately feet were running along the corridor. They stopped at the door and a flat Australian voice, not whispering at all, said, 'Now what's going on here? What kind of fix have you been getting yourself into, my lady?'

Another weak flutter of fear and gratitude and apology, and the flat slow voice again, 'Now what's all this about "doctor"? I can't have words like that coming from a nice lady like you. "Doctor" indeed. I don't know what the world's coming to. You'll be saying "nurse" next, won't you? Don't try to deny it, you will be, and "hospital" too, I wouldn't be surprised. The language you ladies pick up hanging around a place like this.'

On and on, in a flat-voiced song of affection and reassurance. Then he said, 'Now I'm going to have to give you a big injection. It's going to hurt a bit, but I promise it will make you feel better. You might even be able to get a bit of shut-eye, which is not too easy to get around hospitals, look, you've got me saying it now, I'll have to go and gargle with the Dettol. And I don't want you worrying yourself: just you remember, it's going to hurt you more than it'll hurt me.'

She was still laughing when she gave a harsh gasp and he

said, urgently now, 'Good girl. You're a very good brave girl. Good girl. There. All done now.'

He kept the talk rippling on for a few moments more, I suppose until she was drowsy, and said he would see her later when she'd had a bit of a sleep, 'and no more dirty talk in the meantime, mind'. I didn't hear him go.

She lay still, murmuring sometimes, sometimes catching her breath and expelling it in little puffing snorts. Then she was breathing quietly, and after a while I went to sleep.

He did come back. Around midnight I heard a stir beyond the curtain, then the phone, then his feet, running, then slowing. This time there was no talk. Instead there was the subdued bustle and the glow of hooded torches and the faint vibration of rubber wheels which told me that at some earlier time she had permanently vacated her temporary premises on the trolley.

Was it an unhappy death? Most people would say, yes, of course it was, dying alone, unprepared, on a hospital trolley. I'm not sure. I only know her death from the sounds which came from beyond the curtain. I do not know what phantoms attended those last, drugged, dreaming moments of her life, but I think a human voice had evaporated some of her fears, and made a warmer place for her to rest in.

Now for the first time I felt the desire to write fiction. I wanted to feel I could change this inexorable place, these lonely, shapeless deaths, even in imagination: fiction as defiance of exigency.

I also wanted to memorialise the woman on the trolley—to make her a story about a more fortunate mortal who was able to choose his death in a place a world away from hospitals.

Dan was the one I came across first. He was reeling around behind the tool shop at Norlap Tech, drunk out of his mind because he'd made the football team and Sarah Mulhurst all in one day. Dan was a bit of a wild man; he didn't last much longer at Norlap than I did. I came across him again a few years later when I'd been doing a bit of pig-shooting up Balranald way. Someone told me about this maniac who'd taken a baby razorback to Melbourne after a shooting trip. He'd nailed the mother, but not before she'd taken out two of his best dogs so he picked out one of the little porkers to make up. So then there was this huge razorback with tusks half a metre long huffling and snuffling around some little weatherboard house like the family labrador, though nowhere near as friendly and well-mannered. Christ only knows what the local council made of it.

Anyway, when I checked the story out it was Dan, and I started dropping in when Midge the razorback wasn't on yard duty. Though it always came wandering along when we were having a hand or two of cards, and it would thoughtfully rub a tusk up and down your leg and give your crotch a bit of a nudge, and I'd lose money every time.

Finally it started snuffling around the baby with a happy look in its little pig eyes, and Dan's wife said the pig would have to go, so they got an Italian mate in and turned Midge into salami over a long and disorderly weekend. Dan's settled down now—lives down the east coast somewhere. Got three kids, I think. No razorbacks.

If Dan was wild, Noah was wilder, though in a quiet sort of way. You wouldn't believe some of the stories Dan told about him when they were working the railroads together, though I do. Crazy. They had a pretty tough time as kids; someone said their dad and mum had been into one of those weird religions somewhere up in the wheat country, and the kids got belted for every little thing, so they started doing a few big things to keep ahead, and then shot through for good when Noah was maybe fifteen—Dan was a couple of years younger. They sure didn't show any trace of religion. Except that Noah was a bit of a fanatic in a funny sort of way. He just ignored anyone who tried to push him around, didn't give them any sort of attention. He only cared about what he cared about, and what he cared about was not being hassled, and surfing.

While he never talked much—over the last months he hardly talked at all—it was good being with him. He was 'pure in heart' somehow, and us ordinary murky-hearted characters can never resist that. He set himself up at Dutchman's Bay, not far from the edge of the Nullarbor, in an old cray shed. I was a halfway-good surfer, so after a while Dan got around to asking me to go down there with him, and I did, and fetched up staying most of the summer.

At first Noah tried camping back in the swamp behind the dunes, but he reckoned he was at the wrong end of the food chain there—the mozzies were big as crocs and twice as savage, the frogs ate the mozzies, the snakes ate the frogs, and they all kept having a go at him—so he moved into the cray shed on the sea side of the dunes. It was OK at night, except for the smell, but in the daytime the iron roof got hot as the hobs of hell.

Then someone told him about a giant mattress at the local tip, so he borrowed a ute and scored it. He and Les—they'd been mates for years, where Noah was Les was always somewhere about—trimmed a few of the straighter melaleucas, hoisted the mattress up on top of them, hung sacks and whatever bits of cloth they could find along the sides, and sloshed buckets of seawater all over it. And it worked; it was just like the old Coolgardie safe we had on the verandah when I was a kid. We'd sit there on the beach in the dripping coolness, with the heat-shimmer all around, pulling pipes, watching the swell. And when the sea started flexing its muscles we'd surf.

It was peaceful there. As many fish and shellfish as you could want, big crays in the rock caves, abalone for the taking along the reef. The abs were as good as cash: we could trade them for just about everything we wanted in the town. Except dope: they always wanted cash for dope, and sometimes we ran out of our own stuff. So we'd sell the rest of the abs to the pro who held the licence for that bit of the coast. He was on his own, and once he looked us over he decided to live and let live.

We didn't worry too much about sex there—somehow with the surf you don't want it much, or at least I don't. Les and I had regular girls parked somewhere not too far away, and of course Dan was already married. But just about every time Noah went into town he came back with a girl, and they always wanted to stay. For a while. Noah was bloody good-looking—long and lean, with his bleached-out hair and his blue eyes—and even the dumbest chick could see he was a god on a board, carving a wave as casual and graceful as a big gull playing with the sea. And he was very gentle with his women, gazing at them so sweetly, usually because he was stoned, although they never seemed to cotton on. And then there were us other nature boys and class surfers lying around, and the girl would reckon she was queen bee in paradise. But after a while they'd get sick of eating fish every meal and the afternoons being the same as the mornings which were the same as the nights, and they'd wake up that what Noah cared about was not being bothered and the waves and his bong and a screw if there happened to be one around, in that order, and they'd start getting bitchy or complaining about having to go back into the swamp with the snakes every time they wanted a shit, or they'd try to liven things up by coming on to one of us, and then they'd get sulky when Noah didn't even notice, so they'd find a lift back to town. And Noah would come back with another one. Someone said Noah once had a proper girl, for a long time, too, and a couple of kids, but he never mentioned them.

But Dutchman's held him. The surf can be wild there, and it's always big—big surges driving in against the cliffs, and the sea deep and shallowing fast. Quite a few sharks, most of them great whites. I only saw a couple in all my time there, but you don't see those bastards. I know they scared the shit out of me—a white looks big as a tank under the water, but a whole lot faster, more like a guided missile with your name on it. Shark men say they're not like other sharks, bumping before they bite. The old white just opens his throat, and bang, you're gone.

Dan and Noah used to play a crazy game out in the whites' territory. Usually towards evening, and usually when they were really stoned, one or the other would mutter, 'The boy want a paddle?'

Then they'd both be haring down the beach, on to their boards, and paddling out like crazy. The game was to see which one would chicken and head in first. If there was any sort of swell we'd lose sight of them once they were past the break. Then, after a long time, with the night closing down, one or the other—it was usually Dan—would come strolling up the beach, and then a long time after that the other one. Crazy.

Then one day Dan had gone to see his wife who was working in a town not too far away, and the surf was bad, and we'd been smoking pretty steadily, and Noah asked Les and me if we wanted a paddle. Les didn't even bother to answer, but I was just stoned enough to think I could handle it, seeing that Noah wasn't a star paddler—he got his waves too easily. I got plenty of practice, and had the muscles to prove it. I hit the water fast and paddled like hell, thinking I'd get so far ahead he'd give up and turn back. When I was finally winded I stopped for a breather. A few moments later, I swear it can't have been more than five seconds, and Noah went creaming past me, stroking slow and happy, his eyes full of light, set for the South Pole. There was a last flicker of pale heels in the dark heaves of water, and then he was gone, and I was all alone, with night coming on, sitting on a splinter in the middle of the Great Bloody Southern Ocean.

I've never felt so lonely in my life. I couldn't even see where the land was; just these long dark clouds melting into dark sky and darker sea. And then I saw a little flickering light, a long way further to the left than I'd been looking. Good old Les had had the sense to light a fire. I screamed in a lot faster than I'd gone out, and shook for about an hour. It was one of the worst times in my life, out there, on my own, with the sea moving under me.

It never worried Noah. He treated it like it was his backyard. Though he did admit to being scared once. He'd been pottering around out there and he looked down and straight underneath but a long way down there was this huge dark shape, getting bigger by the second and coming up like a lift run amok. He had time to remember a lot of monster-of-the-deep stories before it broke the water right beside him. A bloody great turtle, big as a billiard table. They twisted their necks and gawped at each other, both of them horrified out of their brains, and then they stuck their bums up and paddled like hell in opposite directions.

If the days were great, the nights were better. White moonlight, white sands, white sea, but a still, silvery white, with none of the daytime shimmer and shake. You can't judge distance at all in that light. Once when Les was trying to track a phantom fox in the moonlight he walked splat into a two-metre caveaway in the side of a dune, and reeled around for a while thinking God had walloped him with a huge sand fist. He just hadn't noticed when the white went vertical. The fox must've pissed himself laughing.

Some people say Europeans, whites, have no call to be in this country, that they just don't belong here, but I reckon Dan and Noah and Les were sort of like white Aborigines. They didn't want to be anywhere else but where they were, they didn't want to change anything, they shared everything, and they pretty much lived off the land. Except for dope and a bit of grog, and even the blackfellas traded for some sacred things. They'd got into some pretty rough stuff in their time, but at Dutchman's they were always quiet and gentle with each other, unless they were hassling for a wave. They sat on the beach under the mattress, their hair bleached white, skin burnt black, the salt drying in white streaks on their skin, staring at the horizon, watching for sets. Yeah. White Aborigines, or close enough.

Noah even had that desert thing that Aborigines get wrong with their eyes; something about dust, or not taking care to keep the flies off, wrong pressure, something like that. Sometimes the sky and sea would blur into one shimmer, with little flashes of white light. The doc round at Yorooboola said he'd go blind if he didn't go to Perth or Adelaide and have it fixed up, but Noah just shrugged. He was shit-scared of hospitals, with half-arsed nurses bossing you about, making you piss in bottles and crap in pans; all metal and rubber and whooshing doors; no dope, no sex, no surf.

He wasn't about to go anywhere. He just wanted to be at the bay. He told me once when we were sitting under the mattress getting dripped on that when he was a little kid there'd been a picture in the sleepout he shared with Dan. It was a picture of a little creek running down a mountain covered in rainforest in New Guinea or somewhere. Noah said he'd spent a lot of time imagining his way right down that creek to the sea, leaving everything behind. Except Dan. He'd take Dan. And then at the end there'd be the sea, and waves. I reckon Dutchman's Bay was the place at the end of the creek, the place he'd been looking for ever since he was a little kid stuck up there in the Mallee. I know it was as close to paradise as I'll ever get.

We don't know what happened in the end. There wasn't much of a swell that day, so Dan and Les and I went into the town with a swag of abs for a few supplies and a couple of slabs. It looked as if Noah waited until he was alone, and then paddled out into the long slow swells, and took off his leg rope—when the board washed in, the fastening on the rope was closed. His eyes were pretty bad by then. I'd seen him blinking hard as he looked out to sea, and when he looked at you they were misty, as if clouds were drifting across the blue. And they didn't focus properly: he seemed to be looking somewhere past you, at something you couldn't see. Like I say we don't know what happened out there. I think he let himself drift for a while, lying on the board, watching the sea and the sky until they melted together, and the white light fused inside his eyelids, and the darkness came. And then he must have just rolled off, into the water.

Being able to make a story from nothing instead of concocting it out of elusive memories made me happy. It also relieved my fear of being trapped 'inside'. My labelled body might be lying on my labelled bed, but my mind could be anywhere, keeping whatever company I chose.

I also discovered that fiction can make its own claims to truth; that I believed in fabricated Noah more completely than I believed in my account of myself as a girl. Fiction began to offer a balm for the obstinate opacities, the jagged inadequacies of memory.

I wrote more stories. I discovered what surprising company the

people who grow from the tip of your pen can be, and how plea-
surable it is to map the small, curiously complete, artificial worlds in
which they live—worlds where madness or death, even murder, is a
fiction.

INDIANS

Josh liked the park, with its wide curving paths and its solid thick
bushes. He didn't go there often—he had to be careful to train in
different places—but now and then he'd go. He especially liked the
trees at the Brighton Road end. It was quiet under the trees, but not
too quiet, and friendly, with little night creatures creaking and scuf-
fling in the leaf litter and the foliage wrapping him close in the
shadows.

On wild nights the leaves whipped his face and torn streamers of
cloud poured across the moon, and then he could only crouch and
wait for the storm to be over. Josh liked rainy nights, with his hood
pulled tight round his face and the raindrops streaking his sleeves
with silvery snail trails. He'd listen to the patter of rain on the litter,
and think about the ants scurrying around, battening down the
hatches, making everything snug. Best of all, he knew that nobody
would come on rainy nights.

Tonight the wind was no more than a murmur. Moonlight
spilled everywhere. He thought of the sherbet bombs in his pocket,
but he would wait, he knew the drill: if someone came he could
have one. And then, if he did his training properly, he could go
straight home with no mapping and stalking, just running along

in the open like the sleek morning joggers along the wide paths and the empty streets and then up the stairs and safe into bed, and soon the shaking would stop.

Those nights he didn't stop to talk to Charlie. But if he hadn't trained, however late it was when he came in out of the darkness, Charlie would be there. Charlie said he didn't run his life for man or clock. He would be sitting in the pool of light with the radio in the corner whispering and laughing to itself, shaping and smoothing the leather or tapping away at one of the bootlasts lined up like upside-down feet along the edge of the bench, and they'd talk.

Or Charlie would, and Josh would listen. Charlie really liked Red Indians. He'd read whole books about them in his time, and he'd stuck up a big picture beside the work calendar of one called Crazy Horse he'd found in a magazine. Charlie explained that 'crazy' didn't mean 'crazy' but something more like 'mystic' or 'wild'. So now when they talked Crazy Horse stared down at them with his hooded eyes and his face that looked as if it had been carved out of a tree.

Sometimes when Josh came in Charlie would just say, 'Ho, kid! Workin' on it?,' but sometimes he'd pretend to hitch up a blanket and say, deep and soft in his throat, 'How!' Josh would giggle and say 'How' back, and then Charlie would make cocoa on the gas burner and they'd sip it together in the warm yellow light, and Charlie would tell him about Red Indians: how they never interfered with other people, but always left them alone to do whatever they wanted. Charlie said an Indian would let you drive your car straight over a cliff with him in it rather than interfere. Not like us palefaces, always pick pick picking away ('pick pick pick,' he'd say, jabbing with his beaky nose) and interfering all the time. Josh knew that was true. Mr Finlayson had always been telling him what to do right until they closed the home down when they all had to be reintegrated, and then he came around to Charlie's to interfere some more until Charlie told him to get lost.

Charlie would tell how the Indians were gentle with each other—they couldn't bear to smack their babies—and yet how brave they were, not like poor bloody soldiers marched off in squads like zombies and getting themselves killed because some idiot told them to. (Charlie had been in the war, and he still couldn't get over it.) Indians were brave because they chose to be, and they trained themselves not to be frightened and to bear pain. The bravest warriors would set themselves an 'ordeal', he called it, something truly hard or dangerous, and they'd do it, or die in the attempt.

Ordeals were things we'd think were crazy, like staying out in the desert for a week without water, or sticking big hooks into their flesh and tying buffalo skulls to the hooks and dragging the skulls around until they passed out. But they wanted to do it, so they did it, and nobody tried to stop them. And when the ordeal was over the whole tribe would honour them and sing songs about them, and if they died they'd still make up songs about how brave they were.

Charlie let Josh have the little room at the top of the stairs on one condition. He had to toughen himself up, to learn to be brave like an Indian, so people would stop pushing him around. He should pick something difficult, it didn't matter what, just something you decided to do to test yourself, and then he'd have to do it and do it until he did it really well. And he was not to tell anyone what he was doing, not even Charlie, because people, white people, just couldn't help themselves. They'd be sure to stick their oar in and ruin everything.

Charlie said he was a bit too old to do ordeals himself, but at least he was his own boss, which was why he'd switched to repairs, and he could drink himself blind whenever he wanted now he'd ditched all the people who used to try to stop him. He reckoned he was doing all right.

So Charlie never asked Josh anything, but he let him put green rings around his ordeal dates on the work calendar, green so they wouldn't get muddled up with the blue and red repair dates, and he'd give a pleased nod when he saw the green tick that meant the training had gone well (Josh had two ticks already) and ask when he should start working on his warrior song.

By himself in the park it was harder to remember to be brave, so Josh thought about Indians as he waited among the leaves, and about the ants, who were like the Indians in a way, living warm and friendly in their deep dim chambers, minding their babies, carrying the tender bundles around in their long metal jaws, and then going out under the huge sky to find food for them, and they'd fight anything that tried to stop them however big it was, and they would never give up until they got the food back home or were killed trying.

Then he heard the footsteps: light, padded, but he heard them. His heart thudded once in his throat, but he swallowed it down, and began to breathe evenly, just as he'd trained himself. Don't panic. Everything's OK.

The footsteps suddenly thumped hollow on the wooden bridge over the weedy duck-pond—a stupid little bridge, with a hump on it like in 'The Three Billygoats Gruff'. The bridge always made him nervous. He didn't like even the thought of those trolls. They shouldn't tell little kids stories like that.

He could see the runner now, swaddled in a dark tracksuit. Girl? Boy? About the right size, anyway. He knew he wasn't ready for a full-grown one, not yet.

The runner was coming fast through the dark, fixed on the lights at Brighton Road. Josh fumbled a sherbet out of his pocket, felt the sweet explosion at the back of his tongue, shook the cord into its familiar loop, and stepped into the path.

Black Sheep

It was a quiet neighbourhood of neat shabby cottages and tiny gardens, a little pocket of habitation tucked away in the ti-tree behind the dunes. Not prosperous—nearly everyone still there was on the pension—but comfortable and friendly, with the Bush Nursing Home not too far away, and the Mobile Library stopping outside the general store every Thursday from eleven until two. But, like everything else, it was changing, and when Sunshine Estates opened their big new development at Grey's Hill for workers ready to drive thirty kilometres to the city, the cottages at The Cove were suddenly in demand: they were cheap, and they made great weekenders if you didn't expect too much.

The locals who weren't thinking of selling were horrified. The townies piled up beer-can mountains for the garbos every week without the least shame; their cars churned up the dust on the gravel roads; their so-called 'music' was an insult to human ears and an affront to human decency. When they heard that the house next to Molly Jenkins had been sold they commiserated, and commiserated even more when a family with a tribe of kids and even more rowdy friends took possession.

Miss Jenkins refused to be stampeded. She'd come across all types in her forty years of teaching, and she didn't stampede easily. She observed her new neighbours. There was no doubt they were rough. They shouted rather than spoke; they used the sort of language—all of them, men, women and children—she associated with boys' lavatories; they played loud and unintelligible music; they drank a truly extraordinary amount of beer; and every weekend was one long barbecue. But if they were rough, they were kind. Stella Donovan was always giving her slices of Sara Lee cake and those horrible little party pies (she didn't seem to know how to cook) until Miss Jenkins persuaded her that her diet wouldn't allow her to eat such things, and at intervals right through those raucous weekends Kenny's wide ruddy face would rise over the side fence and he'd urge her to come on in. When her waterpipe burst he was over in a flash to get things under control, and when her old Citroën wouldn't start he got it going by squirting some stuff from a can into the carburettor to dry it out. He even gave her the can: 'No probs, Miss J, I can get another one easy.'

They were good-hearted people, she told her friends, and good neighbours, too. She considered herself lucky in the Donovans. Heaven knew there were a lot worse. And they'd paid a good price for the place, and Joe would need every penny he had for the nursing home.

The one thing she held against them was the sheep. Trust townies to buy a sheep, doubtless 'to keep the grass down'. They had no idea what they were letting themselves in for—they'd be handfeeding for the best part of the year, for one thing. Further-more, sheep were truly irritating animals. She'd spent ten years at a school in sheep country, and her occasional dealings with them had persuaded her that they were the most stupid, obstinate, unteach-able creatures on God's earth—she'd fetched up helping to sling them into the abattoir van with no compunction at all.

And now the Donovans had one. It had appeared when the whole family moved down for the summer, early in November—it seemed Kenny had lost his job. She was crossing the vacant lot for her morning walk on the beach and there it was: a large lamb, hopelessly wound up in its rope, bleating its silly head off. She wasted ten minutes unwinding it, while it squirmed and twisted and made things as difficult as possible. The next morning it set up baa-ing the moment it saw her, and tried to run towards her, to be pulled up short. Tangled again. As she passed the rope around and under and about, it kept nuzzle-butting her. 'Stop that!' she said crossly, 'I'm not your mother.' It bleated, and tried a little double-footed leap. She clicked her tongue, and walked on.

From then on the sheep made a fuss every time it heard her gate creak, and kept it up unless she went over and rubbed the plush of its bony nose or scratched the budding horns. She took to plucking a handful of clover or a thistle from the tangle by the gate as a treat, and moved its peg a few times a day—townies never thought of things like shade. In time she came to like it being there every morning, waiting for her. What a thing to come to. My friend the Sheep.

Kenny noticed, and teased her about it in his heavy-pawed way. 'Seen your little mate this morning? That's right, feed him up—you'll get a lovely chop from him one of these days, hey, Miss J?'

One morning late in January the lamb wasn't waiting for her. They must have taken it inside—someone had said there was a fox around. She called, listened: no bleating. Ah well. She went on for her usual walk, but she felt a little flat, and went home early with the beginnings of a headache. It wasn't helped by the racket from Kenny's barbecue, which started early and finished late and was even more boisterous than usual. She spent most of the day in her darkened bedroom.

The next day, still no sheep. Strange. Then Kenny came loping back from his run—he was out every morning, regular as clock-work, however late he'd been partying. He spotted the clover in her hand. 'Looking for your little mate? Well, it's your fault you missed out, Miss J, I kept an eye out for you all day. We cooked him yester-day for the big day, you know, Australia Day—hired one of those Greek spit things and cooked him whole. Beautiful he was. I told you you should have come over. Never mind: we'll be getting another one in a couple of weeks—got to have one ready for Easter.'

Miss Jenkins looked at him. 'I see.' A lot of grown men and women scattered around the state would have recognised that look, but Kenny didn't quail. 'I'm seizing up out here, need a warmer. See you later, Miss J.'

'Goodbye, Kenny,' said Miss Jenkins, and went on down to the beach. The next morning she ferried Mrs McIvor to the Bush Nursing Home for her regular Tuesday appointment, and while she was there she mentioned her headaches to Sister, who made an appointment with Dr Lawson for first thing next morning. Unlike the rest of them, when Miss Jenkins complained there was usually something wrong.

Miss Jenkins slept poorly that night. At six she was up, dressed in her town clothes, with her black straw skewered to her head. At 6.05, with the sky just beginning to pale and the morning mist still wreathing through the ti-tree, she went out to her car and squirted some of Kenny's special stuff into the carburettor—she certainly didn't want to stall on such a damp morning. The engine started easily, and she let it run: best to warm it up properly. Then she backed it a little way up the empty road, and sat, gloved hands on the wheel, the engine gently throbbing.

At 6.10 Kenny appeared at the little embankment above the road, and jumped down. The car leapt forward. He saw her face through the windscreen, hesitated, then dived for the far side of the road. The big car swung to follow.

An hour later there were people everywhere. Miss Jenkins was sitting flat on the ground, her good skirt covered in dust. She was being supported by a young constable, who was feeding her sips of lukewarm sweet tea from a spoon. They'd hauled the bloody sack of the body from under the car and bundled it off in an ambulance. Weeping Stella and her wailing children had retired to the house. It was clear enough what had happened, though it had taken Miss Jenkins the best part of an hour to confirm it, poor old soul. She had to tell them all about the Bush Nursing Home appointment, about the headache, about not sleeping well, about taking herself off for her 7.30 appointment not long after six to be sure to be there in plenty of time, about Kenny suddenly manifesting in front of her— that's what she said, 'manifesting'. He couldn't have looked before he'd jumped. She told them how she'd swung the car to miss him, how he'd set off at the same moment in the same direction, how she'd swung the car again—you could see the swerve marks scored into the gravel. How he'd fetched up right under the wheel.

She was fretting over her headache and her disturbed night— was it her fault? had she been too slow to react?—but they reassured her: she'd driven like a pro. It was just one of those things. Quick, too; he died instantly. Silly young bugger anyway, jumping out at her like that.

By 7 p.m. she was blessedly alone. Dr Lawson had checked her and said there was nothing a good night's rest wouldn't fix. The police had taken her statement, composing most of it themselves, and had tiptoed away. The last of the scone-bringers had left. The Donovans and their possessions had been packed into various cars and returned to the city, but not before Stella, red-eyed, stringy-haired, had come to the door to give her a tearful hug and to tell her she mustn't blame herself. Kind people, the Donovans.

She looked at the sherry decanter. Normally she didn't approve of drinking alone. But tonight? She poured a glass, lifted it, and drank.

SISTERS

On the days we were going to see Auntie Lall we had to get up when it was still dark. My mother would light the stove to cook my porridge—'always porridge before a journey'—but she didn't eat any. I would shiver inside my stiff good clothes and spoon hot porridge into my cold stomach while she sipped her tea and watched me and the green clock on the mantelpiece. Then we would go into her bedroom and she would transform herself from her familiar morning bundle into a tall person with a waist and a brown felt hat. As the sky was beginning to lighten she would draw her stumpy lipstick straight across her stretched lips and rub them hard together, so that when they showed again they were red with little spikes of deeper red running out along the wrinkles, and the dog would come grinning and stretching from the washhouse and my father would begin to cough as we went out the front door, down the path and out the gate, and began the walk through the drowsy streets to the station.

It was a long way to Auntie Lall's, nearly two hours in the train and then a tram, and for the whole of it we did not speak because my mother felt that once through the front gate we were on public display, but we never saw anyone we knew because it was too early for the council workers, and once on the train we were safe among the wet soot smell and swarms of strangers. I loved travelling with my mother because I would feel so cosy in the heat radiating from her long bony body, always hot as a furnace whatever the weather, and knowing I could look at everything without having to worry about having the right money or waiting on the wrong platform. And there was always the warm tickle low in my belly which came from looking forward to seeing Auntie Lall.

Mum's younger sisters, the little aunts, used to be in and out of our house all day. While they all had their different characters— Vonnie skinny, Pet jolly, Vi pious, Flo silly—we thought of them as 'the little aunts' because they all looked up to my mother, who had brought them up, as Vi was always telling me, 'single-handed'. I would see my mother waving an imperious hand in the air. Their own mother couldn't or wouldn't, I never knew which. Only Auntie Lall, three years older than my mother and nearly nine years older than Vi, who was first of the little aunts, had left the farm and gone to the city when she was not much more than a schoolgirl, and she never came back for a proper visit, but only to stay a single night.

I have two snapshot memories in my head of Auntie Lall before she fell ill. One is of her jumping down from the train onto a glistening platform wearing a pure white raincoat and carrying a big box which turned out to hold a wonderful smoking bomb, a chocolate football stuffed with strawberry ice-cream and packed in fuming dry ice. In the other she is roaring up to our rented summer cottage in a sidecar, flowery skirts spilling over the sides, flowery

scarf flying in the wind, next to a big sleek man in goggles she introduced as Uncle Val. Then for what seemed the longest time she
didn't come to visit us. And then my mother and I began to go to the
city to visit her.

After the train and the tram ride there would be her corner with
the big market sign. We would get down from the tall city tram and
my mother would grip my hand in her hard hot one and haul me
across the road which was always full of hurtling trucks, and there
would be Auntie Lall's narrow door and beside it the wall-sized
barred window with the ruby velvet curtains, because (I thought
this a wonderful thing) Auntie Lall lived behind the window of
what had been a shop. My mother would bang the lion knocker
and Auntie Lall's husky voice would call out 'Come on in, darling',
and my mother would push the door, and there we would be, right
in her dining room, with the oval table and the four chairs crammed
in one corner and Auntie Lall like a big animal in the huge bed
which filled most of the dark room.

To understand why Lall's bedroom was so surprising you would
have to know about my mother's bedroom, and the little aunts'
bedrooms, and the bedrooms of every other woman I knew. The
bedrooms were all identical but the women still showed them to
each other, leading the visitor down the hall and into the room with
the twin beds and the twin pillows, the bedside tables with the
matching lamps, the kittens or the flower print on the wall. There
was never the least trace of the husband. And the visitor would look
at the flower print or the kitten, and breathe 'Perfect. It's just
perfect,' and give a pleased, congratulatory little nod.

Sometimes when we arrived the room would be full of people, drinking tea or smoking or wandering around in the backyard. They'd leave as soon as we arrived—'pretty quick smart', my mother would say, with satisfaction—but there would still be a few raps on the door, and every time Auntie Lall would sing out 'Come on in, darling', when she couldn't have had the least idea who it was, and giggle at the look on my mother's face while the darling came on in, saw my mother, and backed out.

I'd be hungry by the time we got there in spite of the porridge, but while the little aunts' houses were always bursting with food there was never anything to eat at Auntie Lall's—just a stub of cheese and a couple of flabby tomatoes in the ice-chest, or some blackening bananas and a bag of biscuits next to the jar of parrot seed in the cupboard over the sink. Auntie Lall would say her legs had been too bad to get to the market (the market was just at the end of the street) and if we were peckish there was a jar of barley sugar somewhere that would give our bellyteeth something to chew on. Then she would laugh her rusty old laugh.

I'd imagine the bellyteeth as a pair of false teeth in the bottom of my stomach chomping away on nothing and laugh too, but my mother didn't think it was funny. The moment we'd be out the door she'd be saying that the truth was that Lall didn't get out of bed to shop or to do anything else because she was bone lazy and always had been, that whatever hour of the day or night she was always in bed, and that in bed she would stay until they carried her out feet first. My mother would get very eloquent talking about Auntie Lall. But if I said we should have brought some sandwiches she would give me her look and say she would never insult her sister by doing that.

There really was something wrong with Lall's legs, although I never found out exactly what because she kept the sheet pulled up tight to her armpits. Whatever was under the sheet looked one-piece and solid, like a big mermaid, not like legs at all. I saw them once when she had to lever herself out of bed to go to the toilet, and they were thick and grey as an elephant's, and bulging under their bandages. They looked as if they hurt. My mother saw them too, but she still insisted Lall was faking. My mother was always accusing people of faking. Even when they died she'd still manage to look sceptical.

Auntie Lall would have the big thermos of tea Uncle Val made for her every morning—her medicine, she'd call it, with her long, wheezing, coughing chuckle—and nothing else all day, not even a biscuit, and she'd say Uncle Val would pick something up for supper on his way home. Later my mother would say, 'Pick something up! He'll open a tin, that's what he'll do.' Then she'd go into her mantra: 'Tins! Nothing but tins! Baked beans, spaghetti, baked beans again. It must be a real red letter night when Fancy Boy brings home two bob's worth of fish and chips.' I liked spaghetti and baked beans and I loved fish and chips, although we hardly ever got them because my mother said the newsprint came off on the fish and got into your insides, so I envied Auntie Lall. And I knew Uncle Val wasn't a boy, and that he wasn't fancy. Val was a man.

Lall's bed was huge, 'big as a football field', my mother would say when she was describing it to the little aunts. It didn't look like a football field. It looked like a gardenful of soft satin roses. The coverlet was red silk puffed into bubbles, and it was covered with a dozen or more little silk cushions embroidered with roses, mainly rosy pinks and deep, soft reds. Except for Flora's cushion. Flora's was a clear leaf green, with a curly yellow dragon breathing a lot of curly scarlet and golden fire on one side. Flora was Auntie Lall's toy peke, with hot red-brown eyes and a plumed tail curling tight over her back, and she looked like a little squashed dragon herself, breathing fire at everyone except Auntie Lall and Uncle Val. Lall told me that pekes came from China; that they lived in the palace and were always born in the Great Chan's very bed, and that they were braver than lions or any other living creature despite their small size, which was why the Great Chan had chosen them to live in his bed and guard him night and day.

Flora lived in Lall's bed too, or so my mother said. 'They give her a tray like a cat, right in the corner of the bedroom. Disgusting!' There was also a handsome white cocky called Darling who Auntie Lall said was exactly one hundred and five years old, and who bit everyone except Auntie Lall, especially Uncle Val, so she usually lived out on the back verandah, where she would sit quietly under the table waiting for someone to come out of the kitchen to use the toilet. Then she would come barrelling out, and attack.

I thought Lall's room was like Aladdin's cave, and her bed as beautiful as paradise—more beautiful, because my mother said that paradise was pearly white and smelt of nothing but morning dew, while Lall's bed was rich with colours and full of the scents of India or the Isles of Spice. Just looking at it made me want to burrow into it, to hug the cushions and to pile them over my head, not that I ever did. Flora wouldn't allow it. And I also knew that this was not just Auntie Lall's bed, but that every night Uncle Val would unclothe his big smooth body, and climb in under the rosy coverlet. And I realised this was a simple and important secret which right up until that time had been kept from me.

My mother despised Uncle Val. She said she despised him because Val was such a silly name for a man. She was particularly incensed that the names rhymed. 'Val, Lall, Lall, Val,' she'd chant, flapping her lips like a carp. I didn't think this was reasonable. Uncle Val couldn't help having a silly mother who had named him after Rudolph Valentino, and the Lall part was my mother's fault, because that was the best she had been able to do with Emmeline when she was little. I thought she had done very well. Emmeline wouldn't have suited Auntie Lall at all.

It was also unreasonable for my mother to be angry with Uncle Val when he paid almost no attention to her, and none at all to me. After he had propped up his motorbike on the beach visit he stood on the sand for two hours looking like an elegant seal in his three-piece suit and his dove-grey panama, refusing to sit down on a towel, while Auntie Lall hitched up her skirts and paddled in the little breakers and buried me and tickled me silly.

Val was cleaner than any man I'd ever seen, with glossy skin smelling of what I hoped might be bay rum. Even his fingernails shone. At the beach he had reminded me of a seal, but in his house he was more like a noble dog who lived for only his master. Or in this case his mistress, because his main and overwhelming characteristic was that he adored Auntie Lall. 'Dotes on her, the great fool,' my mother would say, in the tight voice she kept for that household.

I was fascinated. I'd never seen a man who even liked his wife before. He'd watch her face all the time, starting to laugh at her jokes even before she did, and when he sipped from her tea mug he'd always choose the bit of the rim with the lipstick on it while my mother's red mouth wrinkled to a dark prune. 'Tea!' she'd say afterwards, 'Tea! You could smell the fumes half a mile away,' fanning her face as if the fumes had chased her all the way from the city along the railway track through the sheepy fields right into her temperance kitchen.

Val would stroke the speckled, loose-skinned arm beside him as he sat by the bed, and Lall would stroke the stroking hand and play-tease his fingers and call him Boy, or Darling Boy, and sometimes, even with us there, he'd take off his shoes and get right up onto the bed and lie down beside her with his big body on top of the quilt and her swollen body underneath it, with their big hips pressed together and his socked foot against her hidden one.

Usually Val was not there. Usually it was just us, and sooner or later my mother would say she would die without a cup of tea and she would whisk out into the famous foodless kitchen to sniff about in the cupboards, looking for biscuits and counting the tins, and while she was out of the room Auntie Lall and I would do our secret thing. She'd give me a little nod and a wink, and I'd climb up onto the bed, carefully, so I wouldn't joggle her legs, and she'd take my hands in her warm soft ones and lace her fingers tightly with mine so our palms pressed together and I'd feel the hard bands of her rings while I listened to the soft rumble of Flora's growling from the foot of the bed. Then she'd slide the rings off, the ones that could still come off, and spin them on my fingers, and give the tip of each of my fingers a little kiss. They were marvellous rings, heavy ones, old, all of them gold, with rubies and diamonds studded all around them. She'd stack them on my thumbs, raise her pencilled eyebrows and laugh silently, and I'd trace the pencilled line along the line of bone to the puckered skin and the harsh orange-red hair at her temple, and she would lift my limp hair away from my forehead as if it were precious. As if it were beautiful.

We would do all these things silently, listening to my mother banging about in the kitchen. Then the kettle would scream and the boiling water would crash into the teapot and I'd slide back into my chair just as my mother came in and banged down the tray so that the milk flew out of the jug and the teaspoons trembled and Flora flinched on her cushion. Carnal knowledge. Whenever I come across that phrase now I think of Auntie Lall, because carnal knowledge was what she taught me: that there is a special love which sleeps in the flesh, and that special fingertips can waken it.

But what I loved most was the way my mother was in that room. It was as if she was usually asleep and only really woke up when she was there. She would keep her body very stiff and upright, but big spots of colour burned in her cheeks and her eyes were quick and bright as a girl's, and her mouth kept moving even when she wasn't saying anything. I was always hoping they would talk about what they used to do when they were girls together, sharing a bedroom, with the other kids too young to count, but they never did.

I saw an edge from that shared past only once. Darling the cocky made it happen. She knew lots of words, and if she was in a good mood she'd shuffle in from the verandah and croak, 'Give Darling a kiss now darling, give us a kiss now, Darling wants a cuddle, Darling wants a kiss,' with her head on one side and her crest half-raised and her little black eyes gleaming. She'd mutter-talk and make kissing noises until you got really close, and then she'd bite you. One day she got me right on the cheek, not all that far from my eye, and my mother exploded. She said Darling was a danger to everyone and should be put to sleep.

It was the only time I can remember Auntie Lall angry. She heaved herself up in the bed and said why didn't my mother spit the meal out of her mouth just for once and say what she meant, why didn't she say kill, because that was what she had in mind, she'd always been a cold little bitch and pretty damn ready to be rid of someone if they were getting a bit old and barmy and bloody-minded, but there'd be no killing in her household, not while she was around to stop it. And—she was beginning to cool down now, beginning to be able to make a joke of it—if a nip on the cheek could teach me not to be taken in by a cheap line of sweet-talk then it was a lesson worth learning.

As always at Auntie Lall's, my mother was sitting straight-backed in a straight-backed chair, shoes and knees pressed together, bag squarely on lap, hands folded on her bag and looking as if a cyclone wouldn't budge her. But this did. She flushed, her mouth fell open, and her eyes, suddenly flooding with tears, fixed on Auntie Lall's. She tried to say something, choked, put her head down, and cried.

Of course I was terrified. It was like seeing a boulder weep. But what happened to Lall was almost worse. A slow wave of colour rose up from her sheeted body to engulf her shoulders, her neck, her face, as she said, softly, imploringly, 'Stop it, Fi, stop it, you know I didn't mean it, Fifi darling, I'm sorry, I've got no right, I'm sorry, please stop.' After a minute she did stop. And we left.

My mother was silent on the way home, and quiet for the next few days, but her tears made me comprehend something I hadn't really thought about until then. Sharing that room meant that they shared not only memories of fun but secrets, too, and some of the secrets were still charged with blood. I felt proud of my mother, protective of her, and sad for her, too, because her tears had shown me that somehow, in some way I didn't know, she had been bitterly wronged.

Auntie Lall never talked about her time in the country. Instead she talked about what she liked to call 'city life', which meant her life in the city, perhaps to teach me about the world, certainly to scandalise my mother. At seventeen some nameless friction had forced her out of the parental home. My mother's head would give a little jerk and Lall would say, 'Now don't try to deny it, Phoebe. You know they turned me out, you know they told me to go,' and she'd turn her ruined face to me and say, calmly, 'They were a pair of sour, tight-arsed bastards, your grandparents, and don't ever let your mother tell you different.'

So she went to the city, and the fairytale began. Within days she'd landed a job at Solomon's Stores, along with Mr Solomon. 'Sol Solomon was a prince,' she'd say, with a sidelong glance at my mother, 'the best and kindest man you'd find in the world, one of nature's gentlemen. Of course I had to do a bit of selling sometimes to help out, but it was the modelling he wanted me for.' Modelling Mr Solomon's special line, imported corsets and ladies' underwear.

My mother wouldn't even use the word 'corset'. If she absolutely had to refer to such an object she'd look noble and stricken and say 'foundation garment'. Yet here was the sister of her youth admitting, no, boasting of having paraded about in them, of being photographed in them, and swearing that her only regret in life was that she had never 'done a calendar' on her own instead of just the Solomon's catalogue. 'He was too much of a gent,' she'd say, complacently. 'He didn't want the hoi polloi looking at me.' My mother's silence was audible.

I used to wonder—I still wonder—what really went on between Auntie Lall and Mr Solomon. She would always mark the phrase 'working for Mr Solomon' with two arch, delicate little pauses, like Spanish exclamation points. Why did she do that? Was it so I would realise later on, when I too had 'matured', that I might find similar opportunities thrust upon me? Was she telling me she had gone to bed with nature's gentleman, that Mr Solomon was only the first of a chain of (prosperous, benign, fatherly) lovers, lovers who had grown younger with the years, lovers of whom besotted Uncle Val was the most recent and probably the final example? Or was I meant to see her own barely pubescent self, as she represented her, as adorably ingenuous, adorably innocent?

It was clear what my mother thought. She thought her sister had slept her way to the bottom. The idea that Auntie Lall with her swollen legs and her hennaed hair was still wallowing in her bed of sinful joy could make her so angry she'd be sick with it for two or three days after we'd visited. For the longest time I thought we would go back to see Lall when we had only just seen her because, while my mother couldn't help fighting with her, she really loved her, so we went back a day or two later to make up. Then I realised there was another reason. We would borrow Lall's coat, and then we would take it back again.

Auntie Lall owned a 'fingertip', she called it, in a lovely dark silky fur, and my mother had to borrow it, or thought she had to borrow it, to go to my father's dinners, which were staged four times a year by the bowling club 'to keep the ladies happy'.

My mother did not want to go to these dinners—she hated going out, she thought it put her at a disadvantage—but she was determined to go because it was her right, and because the committee numbered among its members some of our local aristocracy: not the doctor but the dentist and the chemist, along with Mr Desgraves from the knitting factory and Mr Fordyce from the cement works. She had been miserable for weeks before the first dinner because she had nothing to wear over her grey lace except her daytime coat. Then she remembered Lall's fur, went all the way to the city to borrow it, and it had been a great success. She had queened it all night on the strength of it. But now people thought she owned the coat, so the day before each dinner up to the city we'd go, and up again afterwards to take it back.

Auntie Lall thought it was a great joke. She'd always pretend to be surprised to see us, and she always made my mother ask for it 'in so many words!', as my mother would splutter to my bored sister, my bored father, 'in so many words!' And I had thought each time that it was just a coincidence that we would take the coat back and forth, back and forth, and later that it was a pretext: that after the crying episode my mother borrowed the coat so she could visit her sister without having to admit she wanted to see her. After all, my mother was proud, and also, as I thought then, shy.

Then we stopped going to see Auntie Lall. Perhaps my father resigned from the club. Perhaps the men remembered the bedrooms and stopped asking the wives. It's even possible my mother bought her own coat. I seem to remember a harsh brown jacket hanging in a bag at the back of her wardrobe.

To be honest, I didn't even notice at first, but as the months went by and we didn't go to the city I began to worry. When I asked my mother she didn't answer, but simply walked away. Even that wasn't surprising. In those days adults believed it was wrong—not unwise, but wrong—to tell a child anything about adults' affairs. Everything was secret, including deaths. I still run into cousins and ask about parents, or, these days, other cousins, to discover hostile or embarrassed moments later that they have been dead and buried for decades; that my mother had elected not to tell me.

Of course telephones were also forbidden to children, so I waited until my mother was out of the house to dial Auntie Lall's number. There was no answer. Some time after that I heard my mother telling my big sister that Auntie Lall had been put into hospital. 'Psy-chi-at-ric,' she mouthed, lusciously. The same day I heard her telling one of the neighbours that the drink had finally got Lall, that Val, the great fool, was out of his mind with worry, that he was spending every minute at the hospital. That Flora, left alone on her green cushion in the big bed, had bitten him to the bone. She didn't say what had happened to Darling.

I didn't and still don't know how my mother knew these things. Had Uncle Val written to her, did he telephone? I do know she did nothing about it. I waited, and hoped, but she made no move to go to the city, and when I rang Auntie Lall's number a month later the operator said the phone had been disconnected.

Auntie Lall died soon after my mother had been officially declared demented, when I had been gone from home for a year. When I went back for a day, reversing a dozen childhood trips, one of the little aunts told me that, like her mother before her and like my mother after her, Auntie Lall had been overtaken by senile dementia, but without the violence which was so spectacular a feature in my mother's case. That with her legs so painful she'd got herself addicted to morphine, but weaned herself off it for Val's sake. That as far as she knew Lall was never in a psychiatric hospital, but a nursing home; that Uncle Val had to sell the house to pay for it. That, as far as she knew, Lall had never been an alcoholic.

As far as she knew. She didn't know much, because suddenly, when I was about eight, just after the beach visit, my mother had forbidden the younger sisters to contact Lall at all. She'd said to 'leave Lall to her,' and they had. They were used to doing what she told them.

Sisters. What could have brought about such carnage? For years I was on my mother's side: I recast Lall's version of her story to tell it differently. I had decided that Auntie Lall's teasing had begun in their earliest childhood, that her deliberate seduction of her sister's child—because I was seduced, and it was deliberate—was only the last in a catalogue of other casual appropriations of her younger sister's possessions. I imagined a long queue of girlfriends, then of boys, filched from my thin tense mother by a glance from the long green eyes, a toss of the long red hair. I imagined Lall cheerfully yielding to pleasure, falling pregnant, forced from home to the city—and landing neatly on her pretty feet, leaving my mother to struggle with four little sisters and a dementing mother in a sad little country town. I loved Lall, but I loved, pitied and admired my mother.

I had also decided that both Lall's teasing and my mother's anger were the green living proof of a strong-rooted love growing out of their entwined past: a love necessary to them both which had strengthened over the years.

Now I think I was wrong. The weight of the counter-story is too heavy. Now I think my mother was the wicked sister after all. I think she threw her dying sister away, and took pleasure in the throwing, because she hated her, and had hated her for a very long time. I think she decided to stop visiting Lall and to cut her off from the little aunts because of what she saw that long-ago day on the beach—Lall happy with a new man, happy playing with me.

I think that later she took me with her to see Lall because she wanted me to see her sister's degradation and her inability to provide the kind of comforts my mother valued, believing that I would cease to love her, because that was the kind of love my mother understood: a strict return for services rendered. I think she knew about our secret game on the bed, and later, when it suited her, she punished Lall for it, and then she punished me. I think she was the kind of woman who should have belonged to a harsh religion. That would have suited her.

For a while, after she had been declared mad, I tried to believe my mother was innocent, or guilty of no more than being ill: that the silent explosions in her head had begun long before, the brain scarring, the mind flaring, darkening. That might explain the silences, the suppressions, the rages. Her unnatural heat. But I don't believe it. I think she made her treks to her sister's bedroom because she wanted to borrow her sister's coat.

PARENTS

St Elsewhere

With time I became accustomed to hospitals, which terrify only transients. Once you begin to watch—and if you want to write you have to watch—you see that for all their corridors and cleanliness they are not impersonal monuments to efficiency or total institutions committed to the obliteration of the individual but something more like a ramshackle provincial town, with little clumps of reliable sociability distributed over a network of familiar routes. The kiosk ladies dispense directions and muddle the change at their counter, the pharmacists try to hide behind theirs, the pathology nurses scold and laugh as your vein collapses again, the septuagenarian volunteer in the coffee bar skims cappuccinos across the counter with the verve of a New York bartender. Unregenerate health-workers suck their cigarettes outside Casualty, and the fellow taking you down to Ultrasound kisses the tea-lady who gets in on Three and asks her what's for tea: she's his mum, his dad is over in the laundry, his little brother works in Orthopaedics. Nurses turn into people; you are fond of some, not others. You learn which doctors know when they are being teased, and which ones don't. You begin to understand hospital acronyms. You know the way to theatre before you're taken. The miracle has been effected. Hospital has become home.

Of a peculiar kind. While hospitals work hard at seeming like ordinary places, the effort shows. The wards imitate the routines of life outside, but everything is at once thin and exaggerated, the morning voices too gay, the evening voices too calm. The horizontal people know that the vertical people are acting. There was a hospital drama a while back called 'St Elsewhere'. It was not a good drama, but it was a fine title: a saint in it somewhere, but eternally elsewhere.

We would listen to the voices from the nurses' room. We knew the tall ginger one had a party last Saturday, we knew there was trouble, we knew the cops came. We saw the slight quiet one who never gets flustered running like a bacchante across the car park in a flight of squealing girls. We waited for the night nurse whose hands were so gentle, while his blond flip of hair and impudent buttocks shouted that his real life was elsewhere, elsewhere, elsewhere.

We pretended the days in the ward were ordinary days, but they were not, they were theatre, from the first eruption of lights and noise which shattered the grey cup of dawn through the rackety hospital morning, the vacant afternoon, the subdued clatter of early evening when we lay propped like babies, waving our spoons at our mouths, through the iron watches of the night.

Sometimes I played at imagining that we were bag ladies, rejects from the real world, and that the hospital was one of those cavernous railway terminals like Grand Central in New York; that there we lay, marooned on our beds, clutching our treasures in our little calico bags, while purposeful, vertical people with clipboards and beepers zigzagged between us, swooped down on one or the other of us, and whisked us away to somewhere else. To elsewhere.

It frightened us, all this acting, because we were not acting. This was where we lived. It is hard to feel secure on a set. We had seen empty wards, the blinds drawn, the beds stripped. We were frightened because we thought the theatre might close and the vertical people stop the mysterious important things they were doing and simply go home, back to their real lives, and we would be left alone in our beds, clutching our lives.

It was at this point that I was sent home. That did not mean I was better, or even 'stabilised'; only that the tests had all been done, my condition mapped, and the rate of deterioration found to be steady.

The trouble with magic is that it tends to get out of hand. Writing is at the best of times an obsessive business, sealing you away behind closed doors for most of your waking hours, rendering you abstracted and churlish for all of them. I had become addicted to my laptop. In hospital it gave meaning to my days and purpose to my nights. But as hospital had become home, home became problematic. Friends and kin thought I had been liberated, returned to them from a sinister place, so my continuing fascination with that place seemed ungracious, even perverse. Meanwhile their preoccupations had come to seem alien, even weird, to me. Accustomed to the solitude of hospital, easily fatigued, given to unexplained lapses and collapses, distracted, moody, I had become monstrously bad company.

There was a chance of rescue. Unlike a friend filched first from the social and then from the actual world over those same months by cancer, I had been dealt a disease which held the possibility of a dramatic denouement. My decline had been slowed by drugs. Beyond that artificial extension glimmered the prospect of the transplant operation. As it happened, the public hospital I used to pass every day on my way to work had developed a transplant team with an international reputation. Now they were ready to consider my case.

Liver transplants have been a viable option only over the last decade or so, when a new anti-rejection drug was brought into clinical use. Before that the few transplantees had routinely died, so the operation was discontinued. It remains an edgy business. The surgery can take twelve or more hours, and is classified as 'heroic', solely, of course, on the basis of the operation's duration and complexity, not patient performance: all we have to do is shut up and lie still. (In fact we don't lie still. Lying still for twelve or more hours can lead to the blood pooling, which is dangerous, so from time to time they pick us up by the feet and shoulders, and shake us.)

A transplant is a treatment of last resort. A panel of specialist medicos must decide when the patient is sufficiently ill to justify the risk, yet not so ill as to jeopardise the outcome. A difficult judgment, and for chronic patients a delicate problem of timing, because one's chance of surviving the trauma of the surgery lessens with age.

There is one alternative scenario. Should your condition suddenly deteriorate, should any one of several impending catastrophes occur, you become a crisis case, where more relaxed criteria might apply.

Only one thing is certain. However complex the calculations, there is nothing you can do to influence them—either the doctors, or your body, will decide.

There is, of course, risk: of death, or irreversible damage. The possibility of an expeditious death did not trouble me. If the nature of my illness had come as a surprise, the intimation of mortality did not. Born in almost any other part of the world and at any other time in history I would probably have been dead years ago, especially with my eyesight and lack of technical competence.

Even in our cosseted society, where death is typically air-brushed out of existence, I had managed to develop a reasonably intimate acquaintance with it. A boy called Robin whose desk I shared in Infants' Grade died of peritonitis: sitting next to me one day, he was gone the next and, as I remember it, boxed in a coffin the day after that. Through some odd notion of decorum we were led in a wobbly crocodile to see him lying yellow as a primrose in a white-lined box, with a shiny white sheet drawn up to his chin and the dark curls I envied him spread on the pillow. Could that be a true memory? Surely not. But that's how I remember it.

I hadn't liked him and I didn't grieve for him, but I thought a lot about Robin and his abrupt translation to some under-described elsewhere. A little later I tended two beloved animals as they died— animals whom at the time I knew more intimately and loved more knowledgeably than any human—and grasped that there was no elsewhere, but only here. Then one night travelling from Melbourne to Geelong when I was about eight I watched a small man with his hat still on his head levitating from a slewing car to land with a conclusive thump on the verge. Not being sure whether the dead felt the cold, I covered him with a rug, and held his hand for company while the grown-ups ran towards the groans and tangled metal further up the road.

Those early encounters, along with others less direct, were powerfully reinforced by the unseasonably early deaths of kin, which, as is the way of things, seemed to come in devastating fast-forward: my older brother at forty-two, my mother, my father, then my sister at fifty-four. My surviving brother, three years my senior, has thus far eluded death three times: from cancer, from haemorrhage, from cerebral malaria. With that background I was clearly living in time-on.

It was my dependence on the decisions of others, those as yet anonymous doctors, which distressed me. I have always found dependence hard to bear. The study which consumed my last years of health had concerned the Aztecs of Mexico, a people whose most powerful deity was a monster of caprice. They called him Night Wind, the Enemy on Both Sides, the Mocker. Now I felt that Tezcatlipoca had forcibly enlisted me among his followers.

As I realised that my days for writing were probably measured, I felt the need to memorialise my parents, to try to discover what kinds of people they were before I was born, before they met—when they were not being my mother and my father. They had died close to three decades ago, but I realised, as most children come to realise, that they would not die until I was dead.

Mysteriously, which apparently is the way these things can happen, my mental condition improved, and I focused urgently on the new task.

WRITING MOTHER

My mother was born in Melbourne in 1897, the third child in a family of five daughters and two late-born sons. She was named Catherine after her mother, a 'c' replacing her mother's 'k'. There were no Ferns or Mirandas in those days; they didn't believe in the magic of naming. The MacArthur family was poor, and became poorer when my grandfather began to cough and wheeze, lost his job as a coal-shoveller at the gasworks at the end of the street, and spent his last years coughing and wheezing in a darkened front room.

At that time and for some time afterwards the family lived in rented rooms in Danks Street, Port Melbourne. Naming worked for the street: it was dank indeed, except where the pub doors swung open and spilled noise and golden light on to the wet stones. My mother's parents knew destruction lurked in that warm spill of light. They'd seen families destroyed by drink, nothing metaphorical about it, directly destroyed: gaunt, bitter women, snivelling, shivering children, a bundle or two, out on the street. They also knew, when that happened, that doors shut and stayed shut until the street was empty again.

So they took the pledge and shut their door, trading an intensified emotional awareness, an exacerbated sensibility, for all the shining sociabilities which lay beyond the door. Respectability in that place, at that time, came at a high cost.

My grandmother, despite or because of her steely gentility, contrived to raise the family alone, sending her daughters out into the neighbourhood to peddle the scones she baked in her tiny kitchen, but my mother at ten suffered such disabling shame at going into the streets with her tray that her mother found her a before-and-after-school job skivvying for two bachelor uncles. She was paid sixpence a week for scrubbing out their house, doing their laundry, and preparing their evening meals. Sixty years later she would flush with anger, remembering that. But she would not criticise her mother, because her mother had had no choice. It was a harem society with an exiled pasha they built behind their closed door, a tense world of women who knew they were vulnerable, with the two small brothers cherished, but tight-swaddled in female anxieties.

Coming back from her uncles' house my mother would scurry to the other side of the road, heart thumping, when the knot of genial drinkers in front of the pub called her sweetheart and offered her sweeties and, later, other things. At thirteen she exchanged school for work in a city shirt factory, joining her two older sisters, but there was no expansion in her experience. While the wages were low even for those times, her boss Mr Bucknell was famous in Port Melbourne for employing only respectable girls, and for guarding them well. He was especially careful of the MacArthur sisters, or so the family legend went: he would escort them across the dark public gardens to the tram stop when he had kept them working late, and personally put them in the charge of the tram conductor. Such things mattered in Danks Street. Respectability was all the MacArthur girls had to sell.

Respectability, and the appeal of their persons. Although she never seemed aware of it, my mother was beautiful as a girl, and remained so into late middle age. In 1915, when she was eighteen, she took a week's holiday at Bethany, a guesthouse in the hills outside Melbourne which met the spartan standards of lower-middle-class gentility. There she met a young man called Tom Jewell. Tom was a steady fellow from Albert Park; a Methodist Sunday School teacher who already held a good job in the Post-Master General's Department, and who took night courses at the Mechanics Institute to better himself. A fine catch for a Danks Street girl.

My mother, however, was impervious—or so she was later to insist. Although she met Tom two or three times when they were back in the city, she never had any interest, she would say— flushing, vexed—in 'carrying it further'. Then in 1916 Tom volunteered for the AIF, and was sent to France. For the next two years he drove ambulances through the mud of some of the worst battlefields in that worst of wars. During all the weeks and months he was away his parents called on 'Tom's girl' every Sunday. By the time he came home, my mother had no choice. They were married soon after his discharge.

Later my mother would imply that the marriage had been imposed on her and that her new husband had no more than acqui-esced in it: a matter of conformity only. She may have believed that. She may have been right—some of those postwar marriages were 'arranged' as surely as anything in India, and driven by social urgencies quite as coercive as an untimely pregnancy. I cannot tell. By the time I knew her she had developed her story to full coherence, and tinctured it evenly with bitterness.

Marriage meant expulsion from her closed female world. It also meant physical separation from familiar Melbourne. With marriage Tom made his long-prepared break from the PMG, and took his bride to live in a half-built house on what were then the rural outskirts of Geelong, where he set up as a cabinet-maker. She could not protest the move—these were, after all, the exact and proper steps for a young man intent on climbing out of the working class— but I would say she felt her separation from her mother and sisters hourly. Timid, proud, mistrustful, she had no talent for making friends, nor time nor place to make them. While Tom built a precarious business she bore and raised four children. Insecurity, poverty and a clutching after the appearance of respectability in the reality of poverty meant that during those years she would have rejected friendly overtures anyway.

The business had scarcely survived the Depression of the early thirties when the plant (uninsured; there had been no money for premiums) burnt to the ground. Disaster taught my father insouciance. He exercised his later modest prosperity with lordly liberality. My mother had had enough of disasters. Her frugality became exaggerated and chronic. As a child I thought her mean, and she was, but only because she always saw the gape of poverty open at her feet.

I was the last-born child of the four. World War II broke out shortly after my fifth birthday, and for a long time I nurtured the unhappy suspicion that the events were connected; that I was the natural companion, if not the agent, of catastrophe. My earliest memories assumed that my parents did not like each other. The marriage was not a failure, or not in the dour terms of those days— the children were fed and educated, the proprieties observed—but there was neither joy nor affection in it. By the time I was five my father had been ejected from the marital bed and banished to the back verandah.

I doubt they touched each other sexually from that time on. Later I discovered that physical banishment was a common and infallible form of birth control. A lot of men fetched up 'in the sleep-out' in those days. But my father's banishment spoke of a more comprehensive alienation. For years my parents avoided even verbal contact: it was 'ask your mother', 'tell your father', with our parrot heads swivelling between them. At moments of high stress my father would apostrophise not my mother, but the heavens, grab his secateurs, click them furiously, and go out and savage a tree. The apple tree called 'Mum's Jonathan' was pruned to a dwarfish stump over the course of one especially tense winter.

My mother's weapon was different: her lips would clamp, her face seem to swell, and she would maintain a malevolent silence for hours and days. When still quite young she developed the deep groove from nostril to lip corner which was the outward mark of her inner rage.

Forced to the margins of domesticity, my father constructed a viable life along and beyond them, pottering in the garden with his espaliers and his beehives, drifting down to the factory, now rebuilt and modestly flourishing, visiting his multitude of friends at week-ends, pursuing selected public affairs and possibly a couple of private ones with the fluffier widows of the neighbourhood, to whom he was always splendidly courtly. He let me tag around with him, gave me a pet name (Viv) when I was little, was abstractedly proud of me as I grew, and I loved him, abstractedly, back. As he aged he became engrossed in the heady dramas of local politics. Despite the corrosions of a bad marriage, he remained uncorroded. Somehow he contrived a happy life.

I doubt my mother ever found a place for happiness. She sustained her guerrilla warfare against her increasingly elusive spouse, and worked to recruit her children to her account of him as ineffectual in action and ludicrous in pretension—grimacing behind his back, signalling her disaffection. Predictably, we were embarrassed by her and for her, and did our best to escape her too. She kept house with energetic but angry zeal, refusing the labour-saving devices my father could have afforded and wanted her to have, denying herself and her children the ordinary comforts of domesticity.

Always, she chose grievance, lugging the week's fruit and meat and vegetables from the market in the town by bus and shank's pony, ignoring my father's offer to bring both her and the shopping home in the work truck. Sometimes she would relent sufficiently to dispatch my big brother to the abattoirs in North Geelong for a side of mutton. He'd come wobbling back with half a carcase in its bloodied muslin roped to his bike. She served fine three-course dinners (we called them teas) and grimly washed up and scoured the pots afterwards. She pedalled away at the old Singer, turning collars, 'making over' outgrown clothes. I was fifteen before I owned a store-bought dress; until then a 'new' dress meant one cobbled by my mother from cheap fabric cut from one of the great bolts in Morrie Jacob's warehouse. She bottled and preserved: I never tasted bought jam until I left home. She split kindling and boiled up the copper and wrung out steaming grey sheets with wet red hands on Mondays, she ironed on Tuesdays, baked on Wednesdays. She fulfilled all the observances of housewifery, but with a kind of furious detachment, fuelled by resentment.

In the afternoons she would have what she called her 'own time', firmly closing the door to her bedroom, and staying in there for two hours or more. She said she read when she was in there, but I, crouched in the hall, yearning for her return, didn't believe her. I imagined her pacing and fuming and throwing pillows about. Then out she would come at four o'clock to put on the kettle for tea.

She died at sixty-nine after a stroke. Death came slowly, and by good fortune I was with her for most of her illness and throughout the last three weeks of her life. Our fraught household had never been much given to talking. We communicated by silences, glances, the occasional oblique comment. As a small child, before I went to school and therefore alone with her for much of the day, I knew that her occasional bursts of speech were not directed to me, but belonged to some private conversation she was pursuing in her head. Later, in a long alienation after my adolescence, we exchanged banalities, and even those warily, watchful for other meanings. Only when she was dying did she talk, and then it was still not to me, but to herself.

She talked eagerly, desperately. What did she talk about? She told stories, and fragments of stories, about episodes in her life. Nearly all of them belonged to her youth, before marriage, before children. Before me. Listening, I could find no pattern in them. It was as if she were randomly shuffling those moments of her early life to see if they could be made into some other shape than the one which had fallen to her.

Or perhaps she talked to hold back the dark. There was another stroke, and her memory began to jump and stick like a scratched record. She was ferociously thirsty, and I could not ease her. Water? No, she did not want water. Ice? Yes, ice. No (tongue writhing in and out of cracked lips)—no, not ice. Ginger ale? No. Barley water, that's it, Faulding's Barley Water. I ran breathless with hope and age down the back lane, noting that the blue plumbago bushes behind the Wan house were still there, that everything else was changed, turned along the blank neat road, past the bus stop, around the corner to Geoff's Grocery, still there, unchanged, Geoff himself still there, stout as a cylinder, lard-pale, emerging from the dim sacks and barrels and saying yes, yes, of course he kept Faulding's. His wonder at seeing the tall adolescent transformed into a tall woman was drowned by his anxious tenderness for my mother. His eyes swam like fish behind the thick spectacles. He loves her, I thought, as I ran back. He loves her more than I do.

She did not want the barley water. It was, after all, not the right taste. When she had fallen asleep the doctor explained that we must think of her brain as being assaulted by a multitude of tiny strokes, dozens of little hammer blows. The connections were being broken, one after the other, leaving only irritable trace-memories. Every last bit was or would be affected. Taste too? Yes. Taste too.

Meanwhile she lay restless, never silent. Then her ungovernable tongue began to race, stuttering, faltering, racing again. Her frown came and went like summer lightning. Then the agitation was stilled forever as her brain was engulfed by one last massive influx of blood.

In death, her face had the stoicism and indifference of a Sybil.

Over all those last days, her main condition had been a kind of girlish bewilderment: how could her life be ending when it had not yet begun? Bound from childhood in a net of unsought obligations, she fought hard, but with weapons which always turned and lacerated her own flesh. In the desolation of old age, with death imminent, I think she finally knew herself to have been trapped, and defeated, from the beginning. My anger at the oblivious oppression of women comes from watching my mother.

Or sometimes I think that, when I am angry. I know she cannot be caught so easily, explained away as the victim of her generation, or gender, or social class, although she was indeed their victim. Three of her sisters 'married away' without such corrosive consequences. The fourth, the most loving and most lovable of them all, married locally, and raised her family behind the milk bar she ran— or shuffled around in, on her poor battered feet—in Bay Street, Port Melbourne, a hop and step from Danks Street. An unreconstructed romantic, she wept over the stories in *True Confessions*, and had endless consoling conversations with the prostitutes who dropped in for milk and cigarettes. 'God love her,' she'd say, gazing after some wan girl. She idolised her indolent, handsome, loving husband and her indolent, handsome, loving sons, spoiling them as she spoilt everyone who came within her generous presence. Her life may have been physically the hardest and socially the least successful of the sisters, but it had the sound of happiness.

Does the secret lie in what we call temperament? My mother was not always dour. Someone just gave me a photograph of her, lightly leaning on her father's chair, with the rest of the family clustered around smiling awkwardly at the camera. She looks to be about nine, and she is smiling a peaceful, relaxed dreaming smile directed at no-one in particular and the world in general. I know that her pet name as a child was Smiler. The nickname implies a natural merriment, but when I knew her she had none of that. What she did have was something more remarkable: a wild, anarchic humour which occasionally erupted in jubilant violence, when she would leap out of her self-absorption like a genie out of a bottle. When we were being specially obnoxious she'd suddenly clench a fist, stick it under our noses, and say, 'Smell how many dead kids on that!' Then she'd whoop, hoick up her skirt, and chase us shrieking round the kitchen with the carving knife.

I remember her dumping the big wicker laundry basket on the way back from the clothes line to snatch the bat in one of our summer-long backyard cricket games, and giving her first ball a mighty swipe straight through the neighbour's washhouse window. She bolted inside and hid in her bedroom, leaving us to face the music. I remember one Monday with the copper on the boil she discovered she was out of washing powder. Her 'borrowing' neighbour didn't respond to her fluting cooees over the side fence. So we stole it. She boosted me over the splintery planks, and whispered instructions and encouragement while I scrambled up onto an outhouse roof, made a grab for the open laundry window, hauled myself over the window ledge, skinning my stomach raw in the process, and toppled head first into the concrete trough. I tossed her the booty and she fled with it, abandoning me to the even tougher job of getting myself back on to our side of the fence. She was sedately outraged when her neighbour told her about the theft. She didn't even catch my eye.

Those were the wild and blessed moments. Normally she was nervous of anything beyond the walls of her house—people, ideas, obligations, expectations—which might threaten its precarious security. She knew, in a way that more sophisticated people do not, the fragility of all social arrangements, especially comfortable ones. She never confused the everyday with the eternal.

Isolated when young, she grew more so with age. In her forties, when I first knew her, she'd blush and be close to tongue-tied if one of my father's friends happened to call at the house, while they were visibly startled by the beauty of Tom's reclusive wife. Presumably they had expected a mad-eyed Mrs Rochester. While she'd talk to the washing-powder neighbour every day over the side fence, only the worst of crises justified violating neighbours' territory, as when the neat bank manager on the downhill side hanged himself in his neat garage, and his pale wife called at the fence to say he was missing. My father, being the closest resident male and therefore authorised, went into the garage and found him. The only people invited into our house were the Port Melbourne kin, most of them dispersed by then to duller and more respectable suburbs, who would appear together or severally at least once a year, while we travelled to East Kew and my grandmother's house for the major family festivals.

At first I took these meetings to be festive occasions, with their lovely plenitude of food and cousins, but I came to realise that for the grown-ups they were competitive affairs, with no holds barred and no prisoners taken in the endless comparing of crockery and cake-making and, above all, children. I doubt my mother ever realised that, although afterwards she would be weary for days, and more silent than ever.

Her children were no company for her. Our house was small—four rooms not counting the sleepout, and one of the four, the dining room, was dedicated to the household gods and never used, except by my father in his permanent domestic exile, and on Sunday nights when we would all listen to Harry Dearth and the Lux Radio Theatre after our skimpy gas-heater baths. But we didn't feel cramped. We didn't jostle for space. Like well-programmed dodgem cars we zipped around on our own little tracks, sometimes seeming to zoom dangerously close, but never, quite, crashing. We didn't touch each other, either. Although my mother's puckered lips might approach a cheek at the end or beginning of some protracted absence, the unspoken message was clear: do not touch. Overt expressions of pride, affection or anger were all equally taboo.

Physical violence was not tolerated. Neither parent ever struck us, and once past the covert pinches and punches of childhood we didn't hit each other either. But we were all pretty expert at violence of the psychological sort, and masters of indirect insult. For example, my second brother, who histrionically detested me—because he was the supplanted knee-baby, because I was by nature vile, who knows? who cares any more?—would come stumping into the kitchen at teatime, and snarl, 'Did she' —meaning me— 'set the table?' Of course I had, setting the table being my job. Then he'd sweep up the cutlery contaminated by my touch and hurl it into the sink. Unclean, you understand. This petty domestic terrorism went on for years, never rebuked. Yet when at fifteen, in response to some sotto-voce sneer, I pushed back my chair, picked up my cup of providentially hot tea, leant over the table, and hurled it in his face, the family was scandalised. I think they feared for my sanity.

The war years lessened my mother's isolation, in a back-door kind of way. My father launched a hostel for soldiers in Geelong, and he'd often bring some lost soul home for a meal or, as the hostel overflowed, for a bed. There were seven young marines stationed at Ballarat who found in our house—in my mother—a sanctuary against homesickness. They gave us kids great local prestige as conduits for American chocolates and comics from their canteen. Three of them were to be killed at Guadalcanal, and another blinded. A country boy from the Mallee whose right arm had been amputated, and couldn't face going home crippled, lived with us until he was ready to go back (he was given a hero's welcome).

My mother accepted them all as family, bossing them, feeding them, listening to them, worrying about them. I don't know if there was propitiation in it—ours was so pagan a household that I assumed my mother had no concern with religion beyond a vague notion that Presbyterianism was British and respectable, and Roman Catholicism foreign and reprehensible—but my big sister was in Sydney when the Japanese shelled it and my elder brother turned seventeen in the last months of the war, so she must have been frightened. Nonetheless, I think her warmth to the boys had a different, deeper source: her natural motherliness. It might seem odd to claim her to be motherly, but she was. I never doubted her love: only her ability to express it, especially to her own offspring, and perhaps especially to me. She loved and was loved by small children. Later, she was one of the few people I trusted to look after my own babies.

The war opened a narrow way into her domestic fortress. After that there were often one or two unfortunates—a woman dying of cancer, another old and rejected by her family, another an ex-alcoholic or possibly a continuing one—in the kitchen, toasting their feet at the open oven door, sipping tea, talking intermittently while Mum nodded and murmured and went on with her work.

I resented them, for their tenure of the warmest place, for her tolerance of what I took to be their exploitation, for my own displacement. It was about that time, when I was thirteen or so, that my unexamined feelings for her came to be examined, and took a sharp downward turn. At issue was what it was to be sexual and female. She was in the midst of suffering, and I mean suffering, menopause, in all its worst manifestations: flooding, hot flushes, frantic irritability, disabling headaches, depression. At the same time she was enduring severe gall bladder attacks, with hours of dry retching, and more blood.

All this she endured silently. We were get-to-the-back-of-the-cave people, proud of our iron upper lips. But these things of blood were classified as 'women's problems', unmentionable before males, their manifestations a corrupt female secret. Anthropology can have its personal uses: belatedly I recognise a classic female-as-polluting syndrome.

I had escaped the infection of female shame up to that point. When I was about ten my mother had told me something about menstruation, but ethereally, with not a word regarding the bloody actuality. Instead she had told me a complicated story about little eggs already waiting in my body, how each little egg would need a fresh bed every month, and so on. It was like my big brother's account of sex, all X and Y chromosomes, when what I urgently needed to know was who put what where.

My mother chose to tell me this strangely sanitised version in the washhouse, while she was cleaning a chicken. Breathing lightly to avoid the hot reek of the wet feathers, I watched her hand going in and out of the dark cavity under the little naked tail, drawing out a stringy pulp of something like squashy pinkish grapes, and then a handful of what were recognisably eggs, but eggs without shells, just yellow blobs jiggling in slime. Then she rinsed the emptied chicken—sticking the tap nozzle right into that hole, turning it on full—and shook the sagging corpse until the scaly legs danced. Then she propped it on the sink to drain.

And there it sat, like a ruined person, opened, inert, violated, with its little flab of stomach and its pimpled chest and the skinny thighs splayed on each side of that obscene hole. Did she know what she was doing? I don't think so. I think she had been subliminally reminded to tell me about women's business by the disgust she felt both for it, and for the bloody task at hand.

When I began menstruating a year later I found nothing particularly horrible or unmanageable about it. If my big sister called it The Curse she did so cheerfully, and, as I thought, dashingly, and I felt the honour of entering the lowest rank of the free and frivolous group I saw as hers. But I also knew, quite consciously, that my twelfth and thirteenth years were likely to be the best years of my life. After that I was at risk of an accelerating slide into a throttling net of obligations and dependencies. At twelve I was still autonomous. I was vividly fit, and desired no-one's approval except my older brother's, and I knew I had that. My twelve-year-old resources seemed infinite.

My delight in the freedom of social and sexual innocence must have been intensified by intimations of its evanescence. As the only female in the house—my sister was still away in the WRANS, the women's version of the navy—it fell to me to care for my sick mother. That required concealing the signs of her sickness from the household males. We became conspirators, keeping our sour female secrets together: I would evaporate from the kitchen table at the tinkle of her bell, and then slide back into my place, eyes lowered, with no indication that I had been away. I would sponge her pain-wearied flesh, pat it dry, help her into a fresh nightgown, sprinkle eau-de-cologne about, preparing patient and room for the five-minute daily visit from husband and sons that protocol required, or the less frequent and even brisker visitations of 'the Doctor', who would swoop in, boom briefly, and swoop out after a prolonged and actorish washing of the doctorly hands at the specially cleaned hand basin. He would also crumple and toss onto the floor the tea-towel I'd carefully ironed and folded. I hated that doctor.

Every morning, before 'the men' were up, I would scuttle through the kitchen with chamber pots brimming with blood and foul-smelling urine and empty and scour them, then shut myself into the washhouse to rinse and rinse the bloodied clouts and light the sagging copper to boil them to whiteness. And even then I would worry: would hanging the white strips out on the clothes-line to dry betray our vile female secret? Would the men guess? Would I activate their justified disgust?

The nursing experience was an elegant riposte to my adolescent fantasy of physical and social autonomy. My mother took care to point the lesson. After she had been ill for many days she thought she was strong enough to take a bath. I ran the water, helped her in, left her relaxing blissfully in the warmth, cleaned her room, remade the bed with fresh linen. I had just put some of her favourite Lorraine Lee roses from the shaggy bush by the front gate into the little cut-glass vases flanking the mirror when I heard her call me.

Somehow she had levered herself out of the bath alone, and was sitting on the stool drying herself, with a second towel draped across her. I thought she wanted me to help dry her, but she didn't. As I came in she stood up and dropped the towel. This most modest of women wanted me to see her body, to count the cost of being a woman: the veined legs, the pouched belly, the flaccid breasts, the stained nipples. She looked at me with a glance which was at once an appeal and an apology. She was confessing the real sin of the flesh: that it aged, that it betrayed you. The display was also an invitation, and a threat. You are a woman now. Join us.

I leant against the door, chatted, held the clean gown ready, slipped it over her head, combed her hair, helped her down the hall to her bed. I had begun what was to be a prolonged campaign of deceit. I would resist her in everything, because I knew something she did not: she was my enemy. As were her sisters, the neighbourhood women—every adult woman I knew. They thought it a sweet and fitting thing for me to turn into my mother. Even my sister, who had fled the house to join the navy, who had boyfriends galore, who was marvellously pretty and gay, would in time come back to her childhood bed under the window to be a daughter again and marry a gentle local man she had known for years. They built their house four streets away, and raised a pigeon pair of children while she miraculously revealed herself as mistress of all those arts daily performed before us through all those years at home. Suddenly she could cook cakes, whip up a batch of scones, make curtains, run up kids' clothes. Just like my mother.

I couldn't and still cannot do any of those things. I ignored the daily lessons, believing—praying—they had nothing to do with me. I think my mother realised that my recalcitrance went well beyond girlish fecklessness. So she began her campaign in earnest: I must put away childish things, most particularly childish dreams, and accept my place. My place was to be a wife, and a mother, and a wife and mother here, beside her.

Deference to public opinion played a part in it—this, after all, was what a girl ought to do—but only a part. There may have been some malice; why shouldn't mothers feel malice towards the youth and arrogance of their daughters? But it was, essentially, a calculation of love. Her dread was that I would be destroyed by the world which she knew so little and feared so much. She had a holy terror of 'showing off', of 'putting yourself forward', of drawing attention in any way at all. I rather liked attention, routinely coming top of the class, winning scholarships, playing flashy, unreliable basketball. She neither congratulated me, nor commented on my trivial triumphs. She would look at me sardonically, sadly, and her look said, 'Forget ambition. It changes nothing. Nothing changes.'

As it happened, I could refuse to play out the standard script because my father decided to give me the same access to education he had given my brothers. He believed that class power could be equalised only through knowledge, the old Mechanics Institute freedom-through-education creed, and I truly believe he had no trace of 'gender prejudice' in him.

But from the time of my mother's illness, the time I secretly set myself against her, a disabling, mutual embarrassment settled upon us. Perhaps each thought she had been wronged. Perhaps each knew she had wronged the other. Until those last weeks before her death, I did not sleep in her house again. There was no overt hostility—indeed I think we felt none—but time spent together was slow, painful, profitless. We were as wary and self-conscious as strangers shut by chance into one small room.

What had happened to her? I now think—with no certainty, I

may be wrong, I may change my mind—that my mother was a woman of strong sexuality, and that her chronic anger, even her dangerous humour, found their roots in her frustration. Her sexual shame was crippling. She must have been a most fearful bride. Nonetheless, I suspect that while as a young wife she resented her husband, and while she feared pregnancy (there was one desperate attempt at an abortion), she had never reconciled herself to her total eclipse as a sexual being, however earnestly she worked to achieve it. I sometimes think she came to love my father, though not to admit it either to him or to herself. It was Tom she called for as she lay dying. Perhaps it was that amputation, part self-inflicted, part inflicted by chance and by her narrow upbringing, which made her what she was.

Perhaps. I turn the kaleidoscope, a new pattern dances in the glass. It is all refractions, shifting plays of light on the fragments of memory. Perhaps we are all fictions of one another's imaginings. I can map the contours of my mother's life from the evidence of those early years of patient watching, from the baffled silences of my adolescence and maturity, from those last weeks of talk. Does that mean I understand her? I can think about that life and have certain ideas of what mattered in it, but the episodes I remember seem to illuminate me rather than her. And remember I have assigned myself a double power. I am both the sole informant and the sole teller, and I cannot be trusted as either.

My mother's story is not yet ended. It will not end while I live, because she lives in me. She influences me a dozen times a day, usually reactively: she appears as the shadow of my feared self, the possibilities within me I do not want to see take hold. She surrendered to surplus flesh, I resist it. Her face was broad, mine is narrow. Her eyes were brown, mine are green. She was too quickly judgmental, so am I. I work my counter-magic because I am afraid of her spell: that I will wake up and find I have become her.

I also grieve for her, and miss her as I never did when she was alive. I would like to understand her, to pay her that last courtesy; to see her, just for a moment, as she saw herself. Philip Larkin says parents fuck you up. I suppose they do. But we do worse to them, denying their separateness more savagely than they ever denied ours. The injustice is systematic: we scrutinise them, blame them, then turn away from them, all the time insisting they continue steadfast, faithfully preferring us above all others. And when they abandon us on the whim of death, we are terminally aggrieved.

I cannot tell whether I sound or look like her, because the people who would know are dead, and because a curious thing has happened. Sometimes, just for a second, I think I see her or someone who might be her in my ordinary daily face—a flash quick as a fish, like the ghosts who live in the freckled depths of an old mirror. When I look again, she is gone. In memory I see her sisters' faces sharp and clear, but hers is blurred, like someone seen through smoke. And while I can hear their voices, each similar in timbre, each utterly distinctive, I cannot hear hers. I can make her lips move, but she does not speak.

After years of refusing to listen, I have lost my mother's voice.

My father was a presence in all this, but a peripheral one. He made a delayed entry into my memory, because before my father there was my grandfather. I have been told my grandfather was an indolent soul ruled by his small square wife, who mightily resembled the Red Queen in both physiognomy and temperament. I can just remember her grey basilisk stare, the fat hands clasped on the shelf of the high stomach. Photographs record him as a majestic figure, a craggy presence exuding natural authority. So he was to me: my private mountain, my Rockies, my Remarkables, where I could climb and camp at will. I sat and sang under the great cliff of his chest. Bivouacked on his thighs, I examined the tangled vegetation of his nostrils, I rooted in his shaggy eyebrows, prospected his shock of dry white hair. I traversed the proud curve of the vest, surveying the buttons, and tracked the slim gold snake, heavy as oil in my fingers, until it dived headfirst into the tight slit of the fob. I winkled out the slim closed shell of the watch, and marvelled at the throbbing life coiled so slenderly within. But my clearest recollection is of walking; not so much with my grandfather, whose head rode among the stars, as with his big creaking boots, pacing like a friendly giant's beside my skipping and running ones.

Then, abruptly, he vanished. I remember no sense of deprivation at his vanishing. Children's lives are full of such unexplained exits. His reassuring persona somehow migrated to the family dog, another creature of natural presence, massive male dignity and imperturbable good will.

Walks continued to be accomplished, but now alongside a less substantial presence, and in the company of low-cut town shoes. Those shoes, and the narrow ankles in their thin grey socks above them, are my first clear recollection of my father. Then specific memories begin to prick the darkness, of my father doing things and me watching. I remember the cool curve of the bath edge under my thighs and drying foam prickling my cheeks and chin as I sat and watched my father shave. He took a craftsman's pleasure in it. The steel blue of the cut-throat razor moved smoothly over the sleek leather strop, the horn-handled brush whisked soap to foam in the enamel mug, then confidently, thickly smothered cheeks and throat, with a swift sideways dab-and-splosh for me. And then, index finger and thumb of the left hand delicately splayed, stretching the puckered skin, the long smooth upward stroke, the rasp of blade against stubble, the expert flickings of surplus foam into the hand basin, the splashings and towellings—and a smooth ruddy face would rise like a refreshed sun from the towel's whiteness, with a question-mark of foam behind one ear, and my own face tingling and prickling from the crisping on my cheek. At ordinary times our bathroom was a chilly greenish place. When my father was shaving it was warm, fragrant, sun-yellow.

Then memory expands to spaces outside the house, still of my father doing things, with me orbiting about him. At first I merely hovered—small children, threatened as they are by their certain knowledge of their own redundancy, are drawn to any purposeful activity—but in time I began to develop theories as to what he was doing, and why. Decades later I was to be irritated by Germaine Greer snivelling about her father never cuddling her. In those days, Greer's and mine, fathers didn't cuddle their children, or mine didn't. Yet I have a puzzling tactile memory of the wiriness of those thin milky arms. Where does that come from? I knew my father loved me because of that special name and, even more surely, because he worked for me. That work was most satisfyingly actualised by his mending of my shoes.

He chose to spend little time inside the house, and on the nights he didn't go out he would be at his workbench in the garage. Sometimes I was allowed to go down through the quiet fruit trees to where he sat in the pool of light from the bulb strung from a rafter, carving foot shapes out of heavy sheets of leather with his deadly triangular knife, wrenching nails out of worn heels, or tapping away at a shoe upended on its iron last. There were five lasts sticking up from the bench. Mine was the smallest, and I thought it a perfect and beautiful thing. I brooded over it, and cherished it. I also cherished my rather clumsily cobbled shoes, not, or not directly, because of my father, but because they had been in intimate contact with my beautiful last. A rather remote filial relationship, mediated through iron and leather, but a strong one nonetheless.

While he was a reliable provider, my father was not a good householder. In our street, where lower-middle-class aspirations were manifested in territorial neatness, our freehold was disgracefully neglected: in a good year our nature-strip grass could wave a metre high. The neighbours thrust their fine-set mowers precisely, exactly, to the boundary, to dramatise our disgrace and their despair. Most unfairly, all the neighbourhood dogs, including our own, shunned our shaggy territory and deposited their smelly brown sausages on the well-shaven strips on either side. The front garden was a wilderness which only my sister ever sought to penetrate, chopping her way in at the end of every winter to plant wavering lines of primulas and Iceland poppies in defiance of the giggling jungle.

The backyard was worse. Sometimes, towards the end of summer, with the grass standing higher than my infant head, my father would spare a day 'for the garden'. The scythe was his preferred, indeed his only garden tool, beyond his beloved secateurs. He would unearth it from the garage and spend half the morning stroking it, sharpening it, testing it—I can hear the rasp of his thumb against singing metal—while he explained to me, or rather expounded while I stood beside him, the art of achieving 'a good edge'. Then he would be off, swinging gracefully, straight down the middle of the yard, and on either side the grass would sigh, and bow, and lie down. And I would follow, not in homage to his expertise, although I was indeed impressed, but because every now and then a soft explosion of withered petals would herald the brief resurrection of the dead birds I had ceremoniously interred in the grass. Caught by the tip of the scythe, the small dry corpse would arch into the air, fly again for a breathless moment, then softly decline earthwards. I would mark where it fell, and retrieve it later for further action.

There was nothing morbid about my passion for burying things. It was no obsession with death but a curiosity regarding the efficacy of ritual which gripped me. The head-high grass provided a perfect setting for experiment. Closed to adult eyes, it was open to the construction of all manner of ceremonial ways, altars and shrines. I hung my avian corpses from branches, buried them, dug them up, buried them again, with chants and rituals of my own devising. For a glorious while I lit funeral pyres and launched ashes and marigold petals down the Ganges of the street gutter, until my mother was alerted by the smoke. I discovered Parsees in Arthur Mee's *Children's Encyclopaedia*, and exposed whatever cadavers I could find to the blowflies as local stand-ins for vultures. What most enthralled me was that, however extravagant or inventive the ceremony, the objects of all this attention remained obstinately and emphatically dead. I suppose it was then that I began my lifetime engagement with just what it is that people seek and think they find in 'religion'.

A quirk of my father's helped fuel these preoccupations. He loved choral music and the pomp of large, colourful, ordered public events. He made a practice of attending major Christian events— the Red Mass on Christmas Eve at St Mary's, the Easter Mass at Anglican All Saints in Noble Street. What is odd is that he would take me with him, even when I was very young. I can remember being roused out of bed, drowsing as the car muttered through empty night streets, and then leaning against my father's legs in my dressing-gown and slippers while tall robed men slow-marched in a dazzle of candle flames until I was leaning and floating in a web of ethereal voices. Later he would pull me out of bed for the Anzac Day dawn service in Johnston's Park. Not much later: I must still have been too young to qualify as a girl, the dawn service being a solemn all-male affair. He never told me how to behave or what to expect on these occasions. Presumably he expected me simply to watch and to enjoy myself, and I did.

It must have been some time later that my father embarked on bee-keeping. Again I was in attendance, no longer as junior observer but as a reasonably dependable subaltern, with my own veil and gloves and responsible for the puffer. He would whistle through his teeth, sometimes talk, occasionally swear; I would hand him things. He was not really suited to bees: he lacked the necessary patience, and when in doubt or danger his impulse was always to speed up rather than to slow down, which even I could see was not good tactics, or not with bees. But he was sensitive to their social grace ('smart little buggers') and he took the trouble to construct an observation hive, as I realise only now, for me, so I could watch them working.

The bees from the hive in the shade of the lemon tree were vicious, but the observation hive stood among the runner beans in open sun, and its bees were sweet-tempered. The side of the bee-box away from the hive entrance was made of glass. All I had to do was to drag over a stump from the wood-heap for a stool, pull my cap well down ('bees panic if they get tangled in hair'), slide out the wooden cover—and there they were, burly Elizabethan courtiers in their rich brown furs and ruffs, clambering over each other, modelling the delicate hexagonal cells and filling them with honey or butting down the pollen caps or tending the darker brood cells, and all ten centimetres from my nose. I spent hours crouched down there, watching the bees.

I always helped on the day of the robbing. It was a cruel business—greasy coils of black smoke, the long comb-knife, the comb hacked from the wires in great dripping chunks, the bees' smoke-dazed, delirious rage. With only two hives we had no extractor. Instead we would hang the comb in a great muslin swag between two chairs in front of the kitchen stove where the heat would speed the flow, and the honey would drip, drip, drip into the preserving pan while its furious owners blackened the flywire door and cursed the honey pirates: they could see their honey, they could smell their honey, they could not get to their honey. Our toilet was on the other side of the bees, so for the couple of days the honey dripped we had to go down the hall, out the front door, down the steps, tiptoe down the side of the house and slide into the toilet before the bees spotted us. They knew what we had done. They burned for revenge. My father would wait until well after dark to put out the emptied combs, and they would be bone dry within an hour of sunrise.

The bees forgave us quickly: within a few days they would be clustered on the damp concrete around the gully trap drinking, or fumbling the lilac which branched deep into the back verandah. Later I would watch them grimly rebuilding their violated palace, filling their treasure houses, nursing the new babies in their royal apartments, and know that the vandals would come again with their smoke and their knives, and that I would be among them.

Early summer was the most exciting time, because then the bees would swarm. Sometimes people would telephone my father to ask him to take away a swarm which had landed in their lemon tree, and we would set off in the truck with a hive box, and there would be the dark pulsing football hanging among the blossom. Sometimes they would choose difficult places, inside an old petrol pump or in the crook of a wall, and then my father would call in Mr Ling, the professional beekeeper, and Mr Ling would arrive, long and cool in his khaki, gently chewing his gum, and he'd study the bees for a while, and then he'd start whistling through his teeth, put the box in position, slide his hand in, and gently scoop them out and into the box, making sure he had the queen. He'd find her by the special noise she made. He never bothered with gloves; sometimes he would look as if he were wearing huge boxing gloves made of solid bees. He'd stroke the buzzing mass off his hands into the box, slide on the lid—and that was that. He said the bees knew his hands.

My father was not an attentive beekeeper, and sometimes one of our hives would swarm, and my father would track them. He'd picked up the habit of whistling through his teeth from Mr Ling— somehow it went with working the bees—and we would set off following the dark billowy balloon streaming across the sky in time with his breathy whistle. Bees don't care about boundaries, so we would have to cross roads, my father holding up a lordly hand if a car were coming, which wasn't often, and march down drives and climb over back fences, with the householders anxiously peering out of windows, especially if they didn't notice the swarm bouncing along in the sky. If he happened to see them peeping, my father would tip his hat and point heavenwards, which did not seem to reassure them.

Sometimes I couldn't keep up—the fences too high, the dogs too hysterical—so I would have to rush around like a terrier to find another way. But I could hear the whistle even when I lost sight of the swarm, and I would usually be close enough when they settled, and the whistling stopped. Then we would study the situation, consult, talk to the people if any showed themselves (most of them hid), plan our strategy, and walk back home to get the box and the gear.

One swarm day my father got well ahead of me because he had walked straight through the big Redpath place and then politely shut the two-metre gate behind him. When I came up I couldn't reach the latch, so I had to cut back to the lane and go around the long way. When I saw my father and the bees again they were heading straight for the river, and I thought the bees were going to Pied Piper him straight into the water, because he was marching along with his chin in the air, not worrying about his feet. He never looked down when he was tracking the bees. I knew there was no point shouting because my mother always said my father was deaf and blind to everything when he was following the bees, but I yelled anyway, and he stopped, just in time. We stood on the river's edge and watched the dark football of our bees go sailing gaily across.

When I was about nine my father started taking me on his evening furniture deliveries in the Rugby truck. Again, it was an odd choice: after all, I had two older brothers, and at nine you're not much good at taking your share of the weight of a wardrobe. I still don't know whether he thought it was character-building or if he simply forgot how small I was. I do know he'd airily say, 'No, no, we can manage,' when a customer moved to help, and that the experience taught me an indelible hatred of moving heavy objects—the dead weight forcing you back, corners digging into flesh, crushed fingers, the sheer horrible recalcitrant thingness of things. I won't have anything to do with lumping furniture now. If there's pressure to 'lend a hand', I'll lay on a fingertip, like a blessing. That's as far as I go.

Nevertheless, doors have to open to admit furniture and the people carrying it, so helping him vastly expanded my social world. I think my father may have intended that. He valued making things and delivering things for much the same reason: it gave intimate access to other people's places, other people's dreams. He had gone off to World War I a decorous young Methodist: he came back amiably sceptical of institutions and ideologies, with a developed taste for foreign places and peoples. Later he was to outrage my ferocious undergraduate pacifism by insisting on remembering France, the France of the Somme, with affectionate pleasure: the woman who ran the village bar with such wit and grace, the old man with the accordion, the poplars showering the khaki Danaes of the Australian tents with golden coins. In the midst of what I knew to have been hell he represented himself as a delighted tourist. Later still, I would come to revere him for that willed insouciance.

Returned to Australia in a time of conformity, with new suspicions generated by war adding to the great bank of old ones not generated by anything in particular, he continued his pursuit of the exotic. There were not many foreigners around in provincial towns until the great wave of migration after World War II, and he had to make do with what he could find. I remember him trying a family of Protestant sectarians for a while. He had begun taking me when he went visiting, and I think they might have been Plymouth Brethren, but there was no hint of Old Testament fire or fury about them. The parents looked as if they had been made out of soap, and the children had that sly-eyed skinned-rabbit look of things born prematurely. Their conversation was irremediably proper. Their notion of daring was to make watery little jokes about alcohol. Mr Blythe (truly, that was their name) would bare his bloodless gums and say 'Bottoms up!' as he quaffed his raspberry vinegar, soapy Mrs Blythe would say 'Ooh Reg!' and Stanley and Susan would titter and cut their pale eyes at each other. So we gave them up to concentrate on our reliable local aliens, the Catholics.

For my mother, for her sisters, for almost everyone else who even mentioned them, Catholics were as identifiable as they were reprehensible. They were reprehensible because they had sold themselves to a foreign power: they took their orders from the Pope, who was an Eye-tie. On his orders they bred like rabbits so they could take over the entire public service and look after their own. They had already got their hands on all the best sites in Geelong—look at all the hills with Catholic churches on top of them, with St Mary's stuck up there the highest of the lot. But luckily you could always pick them: their eyes were set too close together and they couldn't look you in the face. The dead give-away was they said haitch instead of aitch.

I knew about Catholics from personal experience. The way home from school took me past St Augustine's, an ugly red building behind a high slatted fence. I was careful to walk on the other side of the road, but I could still catch flickering glimpses through the pickets of pallid men in long black dresses striding around the oval with their faces bent over little black books. Books they were reading. Or pretending to read: how could you possibly read a book with your legs going at that rate? What could they be doing? Spying, my mother said. Working It Off, said Mrs Williams, even more obscurely. But at least they stayed on their side of the palings, and at least there were never any boys around when I had to pass.

And then, one afternoon, there they were, a whole clump of boys, on the corner, watching me. I kept walking; I couldn't think what else to do. They rushed me, grabbed my school case, pulled out the books, ripped out handfuls of pages, threw them into the muddy gutter. I stood there, looking at them as they savaged the pages. I was beginning second grade, so I must have been seven; the boys were ten or more. Then I was on my back, there was blood running over my chin and down the front of my dress, and I heard the thud of their feet as they tore back across the road.

I picked myself up, collected what was left of the books, wiping off the dirt and getting blood all over them instead, set off up the hill again, and told my mother when I made it home that the Catholics had got me. She was stricken, but not surprised. Then my brothers tumbled in, flushed and triumphant. Neither of them would dream of losing caste by walking anywhere near me, but they'd seen what was happening from the bottom of the hill.

They'd had the Graham brothers with them, famously tough characters even at our tough school, and they had descended on the Catholics and smitten them mightily. My mother seemed to think that made everything all right, but my nose still bubbled red, my books were ruined, and I knew I would be in big trouble with Mrs Martens in the morning.

I did not worry about the Catholics getting me again. They were a natural hazard: like swooping magpies, there was no point worrying before it happened, and nothing to do about it when it did. It didn't happen again but when I was twelve, and had two friends to walk home with, the Catholic boys would squint at us through their narrow-set eyes from behind their palings and shout-whisper bad things at us, which was almost worse. So for a time I accepted my mother's view: Catholics, which in the Australia of that time meant the Irish variety, were an ugly, spiteful and violent crew, and I wished them ill and elsewhere.

My father, however, sought Catholics out. He was a Mason, for reasons of sociability and because he found it amusing to oblige one especially cherished enemy to clasp his hand in brotherly love. I doubt the rituals held much attraction; I suspect they struck him as poorly conceived and amateurishly executed. He certainly made no objection when I whirled and pranced in his delightful little blue apron. He was also marvellously oblivious to Masonic ideology, continuing to do all the cabinet-making work for the Brothers at the local orphanage with sunny pleasure, and at reduced rates. We would go out there in the Rugby, through the big gates, up the long drive, and I would be left, miserable and anxious, sitting in the truck under the dark fir trees while he crunched across the gravel and thumped at the great double doors. He would turn to admire the view, bouncing on the balls of his feet, whistling through his teeth, until a narrow panel creaked open, a pale hand snaked out, my father would be drawn inside, and the door would shut.

And I would sit and wait in the gathering gloom. He would be gone for a long time. Bats would begin to flicker through the firs overhead, and once there were owls. Then, after what seemed hours, the door would fly open and he would erupt out in a great knot of black-robed men on a gust of male laughter. There would be multiple rounds of hand-shaking and he would come crunching back with a fruity smell hanging about him, and all the way home he would sing snatches of his only song: 'Where the Mountains of Mourne Sweep Down to the Sea'.

Mr and Mrs Buckley were less dramatic than the Brothers, but sociologically more rewarding. Vic Buckley was a cobbler. His shop was opposite the factory; when Dad went missing from the office we would often find him at Vic's. Vic had lost his legs early in World War II, and Dad, who was head of the local RSL for most of the war years, had helped him rake the money together to set up the shop.

Sometimes we would visit Vic at home. He and his wife lived in a tiny house with a front garden a single pace wide and the door opening straight into the living room. Mrs Buckley was a twig of a woman, a semi-invalid, and she thought the sun shone out of my father. When we arrived she might be tucked up in a rug in a corner of the sofa knitting, but when she saw Dad she'd be up and fussing in a moment, beaming at him, running to get him a cup of tea, digging out her best biscuits. She ignored me, so I was free to find a discreet chair and watch and listen at will.

Photographs festooned the walls, most of them of the Buckleys' children or grandchildren, and they were indeed awesomely numerous. I marvelled that her thin little body could have produced such a tribe. (I didn't think to allow Vic any part in it, probably because of the legs.) Just as my mother would have expected, most of the male offspring of this near-miraculous generation were in the public service. Furthermore, there in the very middle of the mantelpiece was the Italian Pope himself, giving a two-fingered salute. He was flanked by the second Buckley son, who had gone to be a Jesuit. I asked Mrs Buckley if she were pleased about that, and she said indeed she was: the Holy Father had promised that because she had given Him her son she would go straight to Heaven. No queueing for mothers of Jesuits. Then there were the pictures: a sullen Virgin holding a swollen baby with a huge oblong head in her lap, a Bleeding Heart sitting on a black velvet cushion like a chop on a plate, and another Virgin, this one blonde and smiling, with her chest cut open to show her plump pink heart with a thicket of swords stuck in it.

On the evidence of the Buckleys my mother's analysis seemed to have the best of it. Her authority, however, was subverted by our next Catholic household. Even the house entrance was heavy with promise: a narrow dark blue door hard up against a fruit-shop window, with a knocker shaped like a fat golden carp. These were Italian Catholics, and the differences from the local Irish variety were astonishing. True, the Pope was in a place of honour, and true, there were several Virgins on the wall. But none of them had babies—the oldest looked about sixteen—and they were all blonde and delicate and peacefully seated before windows opening on to blurry, luminous landscapes.

Even more remarkable, at least to me, was the actual Toscano daughter. She was called Francesca, impossibly mellifluous name, and she could sit on her long, beautifully brushed dark hair, and even though she was not much older than I was she could play the piano: not the Czerny exercises even I could bang my way through, but real playing, the notes falling from her fingers like raindrops. And all the while there was my father, lounging in a cushiony chair joking with Mr Toscano, sipping wine with dark fruit in it from a glass with a long twirly stem, while cushiony Mrs Toscano plied me with chocolates which seemed to be oozing fruit and wine too. Foreign they were and Catholic to boot, but, I decided that night, all the better for it.

During the anti-German campaigns during the war—when he was president of the RSL, mind—my father protected an old German called Klaus Wittner who had been living in Australia since the twenties. He was an upholsterer, and a good one, and he used to do work for Dad now and then. But as the war news worsened and his old customers fell away he began working for my father all the time, which provoked a scene between my father and a couple of 'patriots' in the factory.

Klaus and his sad fat wife were accused of being spies, first covertly, then publicly. One day children threw gravel at Mrs

Wittner in the street, and one night every one of their windows was broken. For a while it looked as if they'd be put in a camp for enemy aliens, but Dad raised Cain and they were left alone, at least officially. But he couldn't protect them from local malice. I can remember old Klaus sitting with his head in his hands in our kitchen, while my father paced and fumed. In the end Klaus and his wife gassed themselves in their tidy kitchen. My father was grim-faced for quite a time after that. But then a great wave of migrants surged into our industrial town, the factory became a delirium of European accents, and his quick sympathies were bubbling again.

Re-reading to this point, I am disconcerted. I have been offering a little compilation of the vignettes which come sidling into my memory to sketch the relationship between my father and myself. The details are as accurate as memory allows, but the 'Daddy's little mate' interpretation they invite is false. It was not like that at all.

First to dispatch Freud. From my earliest years my father was not the important male in my life. If my mouth dries when I glimpse a stranger with a particular glance or smile or slope of shoulder it is not because he resembles my father. The core of my well-being as a child was the existence in the same house of my older brother.

There was, of course, a family legend to account for our peculiar closeness. When I was born he was six years old and dangerously ill. Was it diphtheria? Pneumonia? I don't remember. One of those vanished diseases with a 'crisis'. Too irritable to swallow his medicine, he was too weak to be forced. So my mother carried me, an anonymous swaddled bundle, into the sick room and explained that as he would not take his medicine and therefore would surely die, and as I would not wish to live in the cruel condition of brother-deprivation, she had decided to starve the baby. My brother, not wishing to go to his grave with child-murder on his conscience, duly downed his medicine, saved two lives, and the myth was born.

The story could be true. It has my mother's flair for melodrama, and her defective sense of limits when truly roused. It is also true that while separately my brother and I had a reputation for being difficult, together we were, effortlessly and always, one another's best.

The trouble with unselfconscious closeness is that it leaves few memories. My brother was for me a state of being; a joyful ambience, not a presence. Sometimes, among strangers, and only for a moment, I think I catch his glance, glimpse his stance (very square, arms folded, smiling from under his eyebrows), but only for a moment. A trick of the light. One ordinary day in Collins Street I watched him for more than a minute when his son, not seen for years and grown to a man, stopped and chatted to his grey-haired aunt. As I watched my brother melted, as I knew he would, leaving only an affable young man and a trivial family resemblance.

There may be other gifts warehoused somewhere in the genes, waiting to ambush the innocent present. Retracing my steps along a beach not many days ago, I saw that my right foot persistently flicked out of line. The effect was mildly schizophrenic: an earnest forward progress disrupted by lapses into comic insouciance. And suddenly there he was, walking towards me along the tide-line in mirror-image, his left foot flicking jauntily out.

It is more than thirty years since he died. Now he rests quietly enough, just below the breastbone, where grief has hollowed a place for him.

By contrast my father was always peripheral to me, an inhabitant of the margins—public places, other people's houses, twilights—between the implacable twin realities of house and school. We were, I suppose, 'consociates', the chilling sociological term for people who occasionally operate in the same social field. We were certainly not intimates. No-one in our family discussed such matters as feelings save with fine Byzantine obliqueness, but my father's avoidance of emotional talk seemed to derive from an obstinately sunny temperament, which I doubt was the case with the rest of us.

Once I had left home, living in another city, occupied with university, then with children and career, I saw little of either parent. After my mother died my father lived alone in what seemed an easy independence of mind and spirit as well as of body—although, counting the years and months now, I see that he did not survive her long. He kept himself busy, taking himself on tours, gazing wistfully across the then impassable frontier into mainland China—he would have loved to have got into China, that distillation of the exotic. He would stay with us for the occasional week and mend odd bits of furniture, with my sons in eager attendance, and then go cheerfully back to his empty house. Or so I believed, and now hope. Then he suffered a major stroke, and, after some months in a cold, expensive nursing home in Geelong, he died.

Through all the years I lived in his house I had thought little about him when we were together, and nothing about him when we were not. He was simply a circumstance of my life. Then, in effect, I forgot him. Curiosity, together with conscious love, came only in those final months of his life, when, at last, I came to pay him the courtesy of proper attention.

My father's attitude to war, which had once caused a division between us, was at the end to bind me closely to him. He had told me something of how he experienced the France of the war, but only in part; only France behind-the-lines. When he suffered the stroke which was to kill him, he was flung back into another France: not the country of friendly villagers and gold-showering trees, but of madness and mud, the France he had sealed away in deepest memory. He was driving an ambulance with Billy, his co-driver, beside him. The ambulance hit a mine. He was thrown clear, and picked up later by a patrol, but Billy was lost. Fifty years later he was lost still, and my father was still searching, shouting, floundering through mud. Only when his commanding officer told him in his daughter's voice to lie still, soldier, everything is under control, we've got Billy, he's safe, did he quieten and lie still, good soldier that he was.

He had suppressed that France not just from me—he talked about other gruesome things casually enough—but also from his quotidian existence, I think because he was by temperament and by moral decision a man of the enlightenment. The brutal mindless-ness of modern war confounded him. Nevertheless, in accordance with his principled belief in knowledge as the way to wisdom, he continued, quietly, to try to make sense of the senseless. He marked his retirement by buying and struggling to read Winston Churchill's massive *History of the English-Speaking Peoples*. At the time a junior historian, I was brashly dismissive of the enterprise. Now I think I understand the grandeur of his intention. In his last years it was Churchill's *The Gathering Storm* which lay most often on his knee as he dozed.

The war—which to me has always meant World War I, the Great War, my father's war—was lodged in my mind long before I took the war poetry undergraduate course which at the time seemed revelatory. Those melancholy dawn services, along with other child-hood experiences of soldiers and their fates delivered to me by my father, had done their work. It is a familiar desolation I encounter in those tiny wheat-belt settlements, most of them not much more than a railway crossing and a silo now, with their long avenues of dusty gums, every one of them with its metal plaque, and the little Anzac drooped over his rifle in front of the closed meeting hall. This country is great in its capacity to contemplate the individual tragedies of war without recourse to bombast, but the best and most enduring argument against war and its assumptions about the essential nature of humanity has been with me, from the beginning, in my father's way of being. He had no capacity for hatred or malice, or for settled suspicion. My mother mistrusted the world, seeing menace in the unfamiliar. My father sought out the different, and looked with delight into the face of the stranger.

He had no violence in him, nor any desire to dominate. It is only now that I realise how steadfastly unpatriarchal he was. My mother would, very occasionally, threaten us with our father's wrath, even make reference to his razor strop, but even as she spoke she was as incredulous as we were, while my father would simply duck his head, and melt away. I cannot remember his ever rebuking, or even instructing me: at most he might make a casual remark which I could interpret, if I chose, as covert advice. If I chose. In consequence, I have never been tempted to take seriously pretensions to coercive authority, whether individual or collective, physical or moral.

I knew him as impatient and quick to anger. I learnt recently from someone I trust that he could be unjust in that anger and obstinate in injustice, and that his insouciance could be suffered by others as irresponsibility. But he was indulgent to me when I was a child, and I am indulgent to him now. I think he was proud of me. I wish he had known how proud I am of him. But that is the way of things between parents and children. When our parents cease to be the context of our lives—when at last they become visible to us as people—we resent their unsought, unearned authority, and resent our submission to it even more. Remembering old intimacies, we are shy of them. We will be able to look directly at them only when death has lifted their shadow from us. And then it is too late.

SNAKES AND LADDERS

DUCK

Writing about my parents I discovered that my memories, powerful as they were, were quite inadequate to penetrate the mystery of my mother. With my less enigmatic father I felt a contrary pull towards the pleasure play of story-making, so that in the end I did not know whether this was my father seen from a child's perspective, or a sweetened filial fiction. Daydreaming about bees seems a long way from the austerities of serious historical inquiry. My interim thought was that memorialising must be slung somewhere between history and fiction, and was haunted, like them, by the ultimate opacity of the subject.

Nonetheless, I was relieved. An obligation had been discharged, and barely in time, because now it was clear that my mind was deteriorating measurably, and by the day.

'Encephalopathy', they call it. It means 'inflamed brain sickness'. It is an effect of the toxins generated by poor liver function. Its progress is uncertain, but it typically begins with small memory lapses and occasional aphasia. It ends in coma. The condition may have been implicated in those early hallucinations, but now I felt its progress daily—a progress I could measure by my increasing difficulty in thinking, and in writing.

To this point I had used writing as diversion, to memorialise parts of my past, as a weapon for the preservation of the self. I had used it to discipline time and to alleviate the loneliness and random dreads of hospital life. And I had just begun to use it to see what I could make it do if I unleashed myself on the heady uplands of fiction.

Now time was collapsing, and society receding daily. As society recedes, introspection intensifies. But how to introspect when your mind grows fickle? How to write when your word store turns into a scree-slope, when memory begins to break up, when whole chunks shear off and drift away? Or you think they do, you suspect they do, but you cannot be sure.

Now I explored the ramshackle mansion of memory differently, pausing on landings, peering down crooked corridors, pushing at half-shut doors; fearful, not sure of what, looking, not sure for what. I found that the poetry memorised from childhood had fled: those rooms were empty now. So was another: once sparsely furnished with a modest collection of other languages, all it contained was a scatter of words lying like broken beads in an unlit corner. How much else had gone? I did not know. And I felt the first stirrings of panic.

Struggling to write a story to catch these panicked thoughts about the fragility of the self, the recognition of the self as reflex of happenstance and illusion, I discovered that I could not do it. I had to acknowledge that words were whirring away like sparrows spraying from a hedgerow. 'Bad' days, of absence, of emptiness, were becoming more frequent. But I kept writing. On the worst days, when a whole sentence-length idea was beyond me, I would try to focus my wavering beam on folk metaphors—metaphors, as I now see, from my childhood, some of them heavy with ancient dread. The death knock. In at the kill. Over the hill. Snake in the grass. Others were resolutely gay: the cat's pyjamas (cat dancing in butcher-boy stripes), the giddy limit (cat ecstatic, gyrating on a precipice). They were vivid, real, solid in a way that, increasingly, I was not.

Then a slither, and I was on a plateau roamed only by single words. At first they were engagingly elaborate. In-can-des-cent. Incan Descent. Skedaddle. Skidoo. It can be quite pleasant, your mind going, once you get used to it. Rip Van Winkle words which have been snoozing in their caves for decades yawn, stretch, come blinking into the light. A word like 'caboodle'. It's a Biggles word: prewar, anyway. Which war? I don't know. The third, the thirty-third, who's counting? The double-winged aeroplane one. The one with zeppelins.

I've never written it down before. Caboodle. Now that spelling's a problem I have to pay strict attention to the sequence of letters. There are some very fine and surprising words when you think about spelling. Like ex-tri-cate. That's a marvellous word, with intricate and articulate both mixed up in it. 'I, of In-can des-cent, will ex-tri-cate myself from this whole ca-boo-dle.'

Then there are all those other words you know how to use but not what they mean. Words like 'post-haste'. It is a Georgette Heyer word, matched horses dashing across moors, booted figures leaping up staircases. Because of 'post-chaise'? Possibly. A lovely word anyway, wherever it comes from.

Message to Self: I OF IN-CAN DES-CENT WILL EX-TRI-CATE

As the wattage dropped, I began grabbing at a word as it flew past, examining it, turning it in my hands. Worrying, sometimes, whether this was sane behaviour, but taking comfort from it: this word at least will not escape me. The word would glow and revolve in my empty mind like a sun. Then I would write down—or print, now my writing was illegible—some of the things I thought about it. A word like 'duck'. 'Duck' was good to think about for a day. The writing could take a week.

It sounds like a duck. Duckduck is better than quackquack. In capitals it even looks like a duck: DUCK. The head curled neatly back against the full curve of the breast and keel, the open U mimicking the amplitude of the bosomy body. The closure of the K at the back of the tongue is the crisp terminal flick of the tail.

There is nothing domestic about the duck, not with those Egyptian eyes. Cleopatra then, queenly, arrow-straight through the water, slave feet toiling underneath. Stately, too. There should be flutes and drums. And then the royal elevation from the water, the slow, seductive progress across the grass, the sidelong glance of the long, kohled eye, the compassion, or is it the irony, in the fold of the folded bill.

Duck dive. Lord love a duck. Vasco Pyjama and his Faithful Duck. Leda and the Duck. I have seen ducks gang-raped and near-drowned by the mob of drakes at the neighbourhood pond, with toddlers watching: 'Daddy why are they fighting?'

When you order Peking Duck they tell you you are going to eat every last scrap of it except the beak. That is meant to make you feel happy, and hungry. Ducks hanging by their feet in restaurant windows, glossy, shiny, red. They look like upside-down martyrs, with their baked heads and their meek little feet.

Duck, Queen, Enigmatic One, pray for us, pray for us sinners. Pray for us now. It will be too late when we are dead.

After more than a year of waiting, and mainly I assumed because of my mental deterioration, I had slithered sufficiently far down the slope of debility to warrant the ultimate gamble. I was accepted onto the waiting list for a liver transplant, or—an alternative, and, as it proved, ironical usage—I was 'activated'. Accepting the congratulations of friends, I repacked my hospital case, settled outstanding accounts. And began to wait.

Euphoria evaporated as I came to realise the constrictions of this limbo. I found I was implicated in a strange game between myself and fate, or the devil. The name you choose for your opponent does not matter. What you may not choose is the nature of the game: it is always Snakes and Ladders. But with a twist. The twist is that while there are lots of snakes of various sizes and degrees of viciousness, there is only one ladder: the transplant operation.

Most patients spend six months or more on the waiting list, and this when they are already miserably ill. They hang between the world in which well people plan, arrange to meet, have expecta-tions of themselves and of others, and their own secret world of perfected solipsism. The snakes are there, unseen, but rearing in the path. You can see the ladder, too, though vaguely. And you know that it may be phantasmal: that the telephone may not ring, that you will land on that last long snake—and down you will go. Fantasies about independence, about effecting or affecting, have long since evaporated. You are not even competent to tend your own body. The clock runs slow and slower, a few memories flap and bang in the near-derelict premises of your mind.

And you wait. It is not possible to hope, because you know everything depends on chance: the savage chance of a brutal accident somewhere in some not too remote place; the chance that a fatally injured victim of that accident survives long enough to reach a hospital; that he or she had one day checked a box or filled out a card, or that a family in the midst of anguish will hear and agree to a barbarous request. That the blood grouping and fine matching will be right. That there is no-one in your particular category in greater need. That the surgical teams can be assembled, a theatre cleared. All that, before the telephone will ring. Truly, Tezcatlipoca rules.

People on the waiting list are always secretly, guiltily tense on public holidays. Road accidents happen on public holidays.

Late on such a day the telephone rang, and I was back in the turning world again. As I walked through Casualty for the preliminary X-rays and tests, medicos and technicians I thought scarcely knew me smiled and wished me luck. Everyone seemed to share my suppressed jubilation. The preparation, in a ward already familiar, was amiable and deceptively casual. With no more than the pre-medication I went happily to sleep.

What happened next I have tried to record as exactly as I was able.

First Day. I am back. I am in Intensive Care. Hard light, the whirrings and cluckings of invisible machines, the sighing of invisible doors. And whispering, lots of whispering. Someone keeps whispering to me: 'Now, Inga, I am going to...' Whisper whisper. On and on. Susurrating. I have never used that word before, never thought it but that is what this person, this woman, is doing. I am pleased to have the right word. I would like to say, 'Stop susurrating! Just do it!' but there is a tube in my nose and a mask over my mouth and anyway I am tired. And I can't see her; she's somewhere behind me, and there are too many tubes, I can't turn my head. I am weighed down like Gulliver.

Now she flicks into view. I can see her out of the corner of my eye. She is thin, pale; she lives inside this underground spaceship. She flicks past, flicks on clear plastic gloves, a little see-through apron, like a French sex farce. What is she going to do? Ridiculous. She flicks between the thick plastic flaps at the end of the cubicle. They are not see-through. They are solid, slabby, like cods' eyes. There is a big metal clock hanging at the end of my metal bed. Its face is blank: there are no numbers, though it has a lot of hands. Or is it that the numbers are there and I can't see them? I don't have my glasses. What have they done with my glasses? Why have they given me a clock?

More people, three or four, tugging at me, pulling at me, all of them talking, talking. Explaining. Shut up; just do it. There is a phone behind my head: the woman is susurrating into that. There is a noise, a vague ululation, deep in my right ear: music? Someone says, 'They're ready for her upstairs.' They start fiddling with a tuft of tubes growing out of my neck, just under that same ear. I wish they'd stop, I think I feel sick; I think I need to concentrate.

Now someone, not the first woman, a new one with hair like bright metal, is screwing spiky plastic things, red, yellow, blue, bright as kindergarten toys, into each of the tubes under my ear. There are a lot of them, they are heavy, they pull my head right over, one eye is looking at the ceiling. They are not toys, they are African earrings, but I am sure you are not meant to put them in all at once. You are meant to put them in one by one, over months, years, so your ears stretch to hold them all. But the woman does not want to wait, she is not going to wait, she is going to put them all in at once, THERE and THERE and THERE. She fans them out on the pillow. She is pleased with her work. She stands back. She says, 'Now you can take her up to the ward.'

Second Day. I know the ward; I have been here before. But this part is new, I have never seen this narrow corridor. They have to edge the trolley out of the corridor into a room. As it swings I see a bright yellow sign with black letters: 'Stop! Infection Control.' It is a small white room with a high narrow bed. Tall machines stand placidly around. They look like friendly elephants. One whole wall is glass. A grey pigeon is flying diagonally across it as they scoop me onto the bed. Hello pigeon!

I lie in my high white room. People come and go. They are all in a good mood, but they do not like my earrings: they click their tongues; they try to coil them up, over my ear so they won't drag so much. Someone is playing a radio somewhere. A choir, male, German, heavy, boom boom. Wagner. I hate that kind of music, but today I do not mind. I am calm as a spider hanging at the end of its silken thread. I do not know the thread is attenuating.

Then it breaks. And I fall.

Second Night. I am a naked worm, skinless, blind; I am a blind leech, I must find a body. I stretch and yearn towards every sound: who's there? Let there be someone. Control yourself. If I cannot see it is only because it is night. I am not blind, it is only that it is night. Please, let there be someone.

The air moves, goes still, turns solid: Carrie? Carrie is solid and calm as a tree. She smells of mint and cold water. She leans over me, her leaf hands brush me here, there. I like Carrie.

But it is Muna I love. She comes to me so quickly through the dark, I hear the pad-pad of her feet, her little snuffling breath as she comes. I snuffle up her smell: something bitter, a Chinese herb, the orange she ate at break. She tells me my name, 'Inga', putting a little feathery upward curl on the end. It sounds light, and happy. She makes me a body out of pillows: Inga, this is for your back, this is for your legs. And this, gently now, gently, this is for your front. O, thank you Muna, thank you. She talks to me, explains what she is doing. We are gardeners together, restoring a garden: this must be done and that must be done and when we have done all these things it will all be put to rights. I hear her talking to four-year-old Paulie in the next room in exactly the same way. Paulie, who screams and weeps through the night, is quiet for Muna.

I know why he screams. We have plastic bladders attached to our bodies, he and I. They slowly fill with fluid from somewhere inside. They are heavy when they are full, and they shift a little when you move. I hear him say, softly, 'The fish, the fish are biting me.' He thinks there are fish in the bladders. There are no fish. How do you tell a four-year-old there are no fish?

There is another person, a man, further down the corridor. You remember the word, the sound, that used to be written in the old comic books? 'Aaarrghh!' That was how they wrote it. 'Aaarrghh!' the balloon would say, when someone fell out a window. I had never heard it, I didn't think it was a real sound. Now I hear it often. He says it, the man down the corridor. First he says, 'Get away from me you bastards.' That is when they come into the room. Then he says, 'Get away, leave me alone, get away.' That is when they touch him. Then he makes that sound. 'Aaarrghh.'

I am falling again.

Third Day. My eyes are closed, but there is a film being run. It is being projected onto the inside of my eyelids. I think it is a film. I am looking at a clay-coloured surface, a pitted surface. Is it just my eyelid? No, it is a film, it is beginning, pay attention now. The surface is clay. It is very smooth; it looks as if it has been washed or smoothed with water. A cave? I can't see properly: the light is shuddering, the camera is jerking about. A bison, is that a bison, a black bison on the wall?

The camera lurches to a stop, pans back, waits. Yes, a bison. And over there, that red, an antelope. Stone Age paintings. Altimira? Lascaux? No time: the camera is moving again. Concentrate. The walls are sagging, collapsing into clay soup. Now the walls are gone, and we are skimming over a clay lake. The surface is sleek, still. Then it quivers. The camera swoops. A tiny split opens. There is a little eye in there. It looks out at me, winks. Then it vanishes. A face is making itself out of the clay, heaving, puffing, pulling itself out of the clay. It's out! It writhes into a grin, splits, plops back. Now faces are bubbling and plopping everywhere. They grin, laughing at me with their wet clay mouths. I am frightened of them; they want to do me harm. I look hard at one and it collapses, slides back into the soup, hides. Then it peeks out again. STOP IT.

The camera stops. It is thinking: what will I do to her next? Ah! It is off again, hold on! The clay has turned to sand, flying sand. We are pulsing over a desert; long smooth waves pulsing over long, smooth, pulsing waves of sand. I can't focus, everything is moving so fast. There is a hump or swelling ahead; it is coming up fast. The camera brakes, a showy skidding ski-stop, the wind whips away the veils of sand, presto! The corpse of a dog, a yellow dog, its feet in the air. It has dried to hair and bone and long black leather lips; the belly is gone, just the ribs and the haunch-bones left, and a few bleached tatters of hide. The long teeth are exposed, and the full depth of the jaws: a snarl, or pain? I can't tell. I don't care. The dog is dead. The camera waits. I say, forget it, you can't scare me with that, you can't scare me with old Simba whatever state she's in. You will have to do better than that.

There is a furious blur like a hive gone mad: the camera is angry. Then it squats down, eyes me. Pure malevolence. It begins to move, slowly. The ululation in my ear shapes itself into a vague melody: some men singing, far away and softly, the barest thread of sound unravelling in the breathing silence. I follow the thread. It wavers upwards, lifts, drops. Words form in my mind. 'Underneath the lamplight, by the barrack gate.' Lili Marlene. Now I see dim shapes. They are men, heavily burdened. Their heads are bent, they are moving very slowly. Mourners? They are coming up out of the ground, out of slits in the ground. Dead men, moving their slow dead limbs, climbing out of their graves? No, not graves. They are climbing out of trenches. Barbed wire loops and coils on the sand. The men begin to run towards the wire. They run with long, dream-like steps, their knees lifting. This is a slow-motion film. They fling their legs out, their pale eyes shine. They are looking at the sky.

They hit the wire. They rise higher, float for a moment. Then they fall. Now they are tumbling, rolling, until they are tight-wrapped in the wire, hooked on the barbs. Their mouths open into round black holes. I am meant to think they are screaming, Oh, Oh, Oh! Their eyes stretch round as their mouths, Oh, Oh! The camera is pleased, it says there, look at that.

I say, No! This is a useless film, it wouldn't fool anybody, no-one would believe it. The camera scowls. It shuffles sideways, glides into the air, and pulls into tight close-up. Panning slowly, it moons into every staring face. It slides closer. It peers into their mouths: open wide now. It grazes their eyeballs. It puts out its tongue, licks delicately, there is the taste of salt in my mouth. *Jesus.* Stop. Stop. Stop *now.* You can't scare me with your lousy film. It's stupid, anyway, you can't do trench warfare in a desert. For trenches you need mud.

I say it, and the mud comes, great sleek waves of it, engulfing everything. Now the men in the wire are floundering, drowning, basting themselves with mud, turning into mud. Their eyes and mouths are full of mud, their arms and legs move like eels under the smooth clay skin. The mud belches and heaves. Horses are screaming off camera, somewhere to the left. That's not fair, you shouldn't use horses, you shouldn't bring horses in. The camera sniggers.

A line of stretcher-bearers is trotting past. The stretchers are heavy, you can see from the men's hunched shoulders, their jerking heads. A pair jogs past me. Their stretcher is empty, the body has slipped off, I can see it, there, in the mud, but they do not know it is empty, that they are jog-jogging to no purpose, because they are blind. One of them lifts his head as he passes, the face swings towards me. His eye sockets are empty, but I know him. I know him. He is my father.

Fourth Day. My eyes are open. I can see the walls, the window. No pigeons. There are people in the corridor, Jenny, and a man, Frank I think.

The film has stopped, but the Germans are still singing deep in my ear, and full volume now. It's Wagner again, I don't know the phrase, but I know it's Wagner, one great straining phrase repeating itself, over and over, always the same, moaning and straining. I hate Wagner, with his stupid fat phoney climaxes. But now it is daylight, so why can I still hear the music? They must be real after all, they must be in the bathroom, there must be ten or more German soldiers singing in my bathroom. Are they really there? I was hallucinating in the night, but I shouldn't be now, not in daylight, not with people just outside in the corridor.

I can be sly too. I wait for the nurse. It's Carrie with her fresh-water smell. I ask her is there a radio somewhere, the music is bothering me, could she please have them turn it down? She says there is no radio, but if the music is bothering me—does that mean she can hear it, too?— I should put on my headphones. She looks for them, finds them in the drawer, fits them on her head, smiles, and says, 'You're in luck. It's the Duke.' She lifts my earrings, carefully slips the headphones over my ears (they are warm from her ears) and it is. It is the Duke. Mood Indigo. Sweet Jesus, it is the Duke.

The Duke smiles and sways, weaving his casual magic. I can hear the Germans in the background: they are faltering, trying to regroup. The Duke tosses a long, curving necklace of notes, catches it, tosses it higher. He is winning, he is forcing them back, he is winning, he will win. I fumble for the tiny knob, find it, turn the volume HIGH.

I have realised something. I must get this clear before the dark comes again. That yellow dog. That was Simba. It is true that she trusted me, and I had her killed. But I am not guilty because she was dying, she was in pain. She wasn't frightened, old Simby; I was holding her when she died—sneezed, and died. The trenches, the stretcher-bearers. The mud, coming just when it did, when I said it should. I know too much about these scripts. They are doing this to me, but I am helping them; I am watching, but I am also behind the camera. I do not control it, I cannot control it, but I am there. Somewhere.

I must get control of the script. But how can I, when I am so tired? And how can I concentrate with this damned music going in my head?

Then I see the boy in the corner. He's young, only about seventeen, in uniform, with a rifle and a knapsack, and he is slumped in the corner under the window. He is German, and he is exhausted. His face is yellow. He could be bleeding, but I can't see any blood.

Our eyes lock. He looks at me with terrible collusive intimacy as if the skin of our eyes is pressed together: please, don't tell them, please, let me rest for a while. I can see the pale stubble on his chin, smell the wet woollen smell of his uniform. This is the worst vision of all, because he is slumped there, I can see him, I can smell him, but I think he is not real. Carrie did not see him.

Or did she see him, and say nothing?

I stare at the boy, he stares at me. Then the Germans shout, and he is gone. There is only the shining floor, the light from the window, the empty corner.

Fourth Night. The camera is back. I thought it had gone, but it was only resting. Waiting. It dances about, jumping at me, pretending to be glad to see me. Off again.

It is dark now, and windy. We are flying over a plain. There is a city, with walls around it. Medieval? Chinese? I can't tell, I can't recognise anything, what is this script? Concentrate. A big city: there are thoroughfares, arches, stone columns. But there are no people. The camera swivels, points: yes, I see, there are some people, over there; as we swoop towards them they scuttle like cockroaches, they vanish into cracks. There is a castle, or palace, with banners, red and gold. There are black signs on them, arabesques. Or dragons; they might be dragons.

We are descending now, hovering, at the entrance, over the forecourt. The great jade doors are levered apart, and in front, on the stairs, there is a pile of metal. It is not as rigid as metal. Flesh? They are men, men in iron; are they drunk, or dead? The camera prances over, sniffs at a rusted corselet. Not rust, blood. Dead. A pile of men in armour, dead.

We don't care; we float up the wide azure stairs, slide through the doors, drift through the reception rooms. The mother-of-pearl walls are hung with tapestries of every-colour silk; they throb in the wind of our passing. Statues stand at intervals. Their hands are empty. They should hold flowers, or torches. All the rooms are empty. No courtiers, no attendants—nobody.

At last, in the centre of a great octagonal room, there are bowlegged men in loincloths, squatting around a fire. They are roasting some small animal: there is a stench of scorching hair and flesh.

They are burning the furniture: delicate wooden legs lie around like antelope bones.

The camera sniffs, picks up its skirts, and whirls into the private apartments. They are empty too. No-one has lived here for months. Dust is thick on the gilded mouldings, the great beds are stripped, the dragon bedposts guard nothing. We prowl, peering, sniffing. Nothing.

Down the staircase again, out to the working parts of the palace. No-one is working, but I can hear shouts, screams, from the kitchens and cellars, and the narrow space between the battlements and the walls is crammed with people. They are peacocking like gipsies in wraps and turbans and skirts of silk, torn from the tapestries on the walls, and they are all drunk. The palace has been looted by its own people.

Then I see him. They have forced him up onto the parapet and forgotten about him. He has no clothes, the emperor has no clothes at all. His wrinkled hide is bare, except for a few tatters of silk clinging to the shrunken buttocks. The wind is tugging at them; it will soon have them off him. He is shuffling from one bloodied, yellow foot to the other, turning slowly, revolving, gazing into the night sky. He is dancing for the moon. He is quite, quite mad.

More shouts from below, more wails, not all from women, and the clang of weapons: an attack? The camera leaps over the parapet, thrusts itself into the fray, come on! Men-at-arms are reeling, whacking at one another: huge, iron-clad, black-cloaked Darth Vaders, whacking and whacking like mechanical monsters. But no-one is falling: they lurch and whack, lurch and whack. At last a monstrous giant sags, is clubbed to the ground, whack, whack, whack. Blood dribbles through the metal casing; the clanking carcase is lugged away. And five huge warriors, identical, in identical dark armour, come lumbering out. To take his place. More shapes rise to meet them: whack, whack, whack.

This battle will never end. It is not intended that this battle should end. An ending is not in the script.

The camera is bored. It jiggles about, scratches itself. Then it wanders away, away from the thuds and the clangs. We are in the kitchen garden now, I can smell the rosemary and the lavender. From here the battle sounds like a Chinese opera, all cymbals and flutes and drums. The stars are out. The camera sits down beside me, nuzzles my hand. It is feeling friendly: it leans against me, shuts its eyes, goes to sleep. I sleep too.

A young colleague has sent me flowers: a tall construction of spiky proteas, topped by the azure and flame spears of strelitzias, bird of paradise flowers. When they brought me up from Intensive Care they were there, floating on a high shelf like an Aztec warrior's war crest.

As I drift in and out of consciousness, I see them, floating.

Now I remember the tiger. I invoke the tiger. I see his black-barred face, his golden eyes. Stiffen the sinew. Summon up the blood. Concentrate.

I am making these dream-stories. I do not choose them, they terrify me, I think they might kill me. Nevertheless, I am making them. This must be what they call paranoia, these visions. To stop them unspooling I must understand why I am making them, and what I am making them from.

The cave. I don't know. I have seen the caves at Altimira. I don't see why they should matter. The dog is Simba. The trenches. My father was in France, he drove an ambulance, therefore the stretcher-bearers. I was angry with him because he would not say war was terrible, when I had read about it and knew that it was. But I had known that before, a long time before. I already knew it was terrible, and that was why I was angry. How did I know that it was terrible?

The other film, the war in the ruined palace. Is it my ruined body, its people rioting through the halls? Mother-of-pearl walls. The mindless, endless battle. The drugs? I don't know. I am tired now, tired of thinking. Concentrate. The bare-arsed old emperor on the parapet, who is he? My mind? My self?

No. I am not the emperor. If I am there at all, I am one of those shreds of silk, streaming, tearing in the wind.

I do not think the film will come back. Sleep now.

Fifth Day. Today the nurses arrange me in the chair, 'just for ten minutes'. They have taken away my African earrings: only one plug, the yellow one, is left, dangling at the end of its plastic. I fumble through my first shower, carefully lifting the other tubes sprouting from under my breasts to wash, careful not to look down, not to look in the mirror. Today I have my first non-family visitor. She is reassured. She says, 'How wonderful! You are yourself again.'

I am not. I am held together by shadow knitting.

Sixth Day, Seventh Day. Everyone is saying how well I am; that I will be able to go home soon. It is true I am better. All the tubes are gone except for one to the bile duct, and that will come home with me. I walk for kilometres around the corridors: my record is five kilometres in one morning. But I still seem to have no skin; I respond to everything. And so irritable. I scribble great lists, of what I must do, of what other people must do. And I talk. I listen to myself talking. I sound like a megalomaniac. I think I am out of control.

They say that all this time I have been on a high from the bolus of drugs they gave me during the operation. That is why I have been so frantic. They say it happens to everyone. Now I have crashed, and that happens to everyone too. In time, I will pick myself up. They say.

I have been thinking about the mud film, the 1914 war. My father's war. Before I knew about his war I knew about the other war, because of the Americans we adopted, the marines my mother adopted, when I was…seven? I could write by then, so about seven. Mickey Espejo and the others, members of the family, part of the household. 'They are only boys,' my mother would say, 'only babies.' Her pet Mickey looked like a baby, a soft brown smiling baby. The one I liked was Steve. Steve Wresser. I used to write to him when they were in the training camp at Ballarat, and he would write back. Then they went to a place called Guadalcanal. Three of them came home. One of them, Eightball, was blind, and Mickey didn't look like a baby any more. Steve Wresser, the one I used to write to and who always wrote back, was dead, killed there somehow. They had photographs of the place. It looked muddy. I have not thought of him for years, but I have never forgotten him. I can see him now, although he has been dead for half a century. Hello Steve. I named my first son Stephen, I thought for other reasons, but perhaps it was for you.

After you were dead, I could not bear to watch the soldiers marching along Noble Street, with the people waving and smiling. My mother would be there too. With her little flag, waving. She knew what they were going to do to you, to them, but she still waved her flag. My mother, my undemonstrative mother, who had looked at Mickey on the day he came back to her door, and took his face in her hands, and pulled his head against her breast, and held it there until he started to cry, held it there until he had stopped crying. Perhaps I have spent my life trying to understand that.

I go home tomorrow, just for a few hours, to get used to it. Then the next day, just for a few hours. Then for good. For good.

Fourteenth Day. There has been a setback. I have had a golden staph infection, but I will be home soon. Perhaps tomorrow.

Later. I must tell you something. On the day I was discharged from the hospital, the day I left the ward, I heard the man down the corridor say something in an ordinary voice. He had never done that before. There had only been shouts and screams. He said, quietly, perhaps to someone in his room, perhaps to nobody, 'Help me. I am being held here against my will.' The person, if there was one, asked him why he thought that, why was he being held? He answered softly, hopelessly, wearily, 'I don't know.'

As I write this he is still there, still lost in a place of terrors. Truly, Tezcatlipoca rules.

HOME

I have been home for two months now. It was strange for a while; now I am used to it. The music followed me from the hospital, lingered for a few days. It was especially loud in the bathroom. Now it has gone. The voices and the eyes of people around me say, 'You have come back to us.' I nod, and smile. They have begun to have expectations of me.

They will be disappointed, because I am different now, now that I know what I am made of. Not sugar, not spice, not snips, not snails. Not pretty tales, either. Just a ragbag of metaphors, a hank of memories and a habit of interrogation, held together by drugs. And if you say 'Aha! what then is this observing and commenting "I"?', I answer that it is a shred, a nothing: a sliver of shattered silk whirling in the wind, without anchor or destiny, surviving only because the wind happened to drop.

These things happened. Then, against the odds, I was home again, with unmeasured time stretching ahead. How was I to make sense of a gratuitous future? Only by making sense of this retrieved self.

As memory and vocabulary failed, I had exchanged writing for introspection. Then came the transplant, and the involuntary introspection of the hallucinations, which came out of my mind and my memory, but from, as it were, the unauthorised version.

Later I asked some fellow-transplantees whether they had hallucinated. A tough-minded cow cocky admitted to half a day of 'bloody stupid dreams', but he had given them short shrift. Others said there had been a few minor visual disturbances, the odd blob and flash, nothing more. The man down the corridor must have been hallucinating. I have to assume that my elaborate orchestrations were peculiar to me—and to the man down the hall.

The hallucinations were dramatic, paranoid, and in both content and style unfamiliar to me. I had no sense of having made them. Initially helpless before them, I could detach myself from them only by turning moving images into words. The silent movies in my head had to be made into a script. Then I could identify them, analyse them, and reclaim them as mine by tracing them back to a previously unconsidered past. Then I would be able to read the cryptic history of the unknown self which had unspooled behind my eyelids. I recognised that here I was in the world of history again, not fiction. I did not 'invent' the hallucinations. These communiqués from my dark interior had long existed, like ancient flints, deep inside me. Now they had worked their way to the light. Only by playing historian to my nightmares would I be able to negate their power.

Analysed, they told me several things I had not known. They explained why I do the kind of history I do: why a middle-class female pacifist and practising atheist should choose to spend her time reflecting on pre-modern warriors, militant clerics and the extreme, indiscriminate violence of holocausts. They told me that the idea of ordinary men being sent or voluntarily going into violent situations of extreme moral challenge and possible death had worried me for a very long time.

I also learnt more about memory, and about history. When I wrote about my mother and father I wanted not so much to memorialise or to honour them, although I intended both, as to see them more clearly before I too was dead. That much I did. But I also knew that I could see them only narrowly, in the close-angled squint of my personal relationship to them. I could not see my mother as a young girl, my father as a schoolboy; I could not see them as the lovers they must once have been, however briefly. I could not see them as they were before I existed—yet that is how I had seen all those other people I had engaged with as a historian. Why was I willing to see strangers in the round—but not my parents, whom I knew intimately, if years count for anything? Was it lack of information? For much of their lives I had only family rumour to go on. Was it the natural opacity of others, clearest and most baffling when seen close up? Was it a willed refusal of insight—the comfortable blindness which sustains domestic intimacies?

Being ill had taught me how much of ourselves there is in all the stories we tell about the past. I had also begun to see the multiple barriers to understanding between ourselves and enigmatic others, and how fiction invites us to overleap those barriers. And I was beginning to suspect, after my drug-induced thrashings and wallowings, that we are fictions too: not coherent and continuous objects in a changing sea, but half-illusory creatures made out of the light and shadows cast by that sea, articulated by our own flickering imaginations. That the Other begins not at the skin, as I had thought, but within.

Then I met Mr Robinson.

READING MR ROBINSON

I grew up in a once-upon-a-time land when milk and loaves appeared at the door to the jingle of bells and the clopping of hooves, when housewives were Cinderellas in sacking aprons and hair permanently rollered for the ball, when men wore hats, and lifted them to the funerals of strangers passing in the street. That time—the forties, the early fifties—has been mythologised into a Camelot of Anglo-Celtic virtue, or a dark age of tribalism and British cooking. In my recollection, of course, it was neither, but simply the way things were. It is disconcerting to find one's private past, one's collection of ordinary memories, become a matter of ideological dispute, and to discover, after peaceful decades spent reading historical documents, that you have become a historical document yourself.

The elevation is the more disconcerting because I know almost nothing of the history of which I have now become an artefact, having abandoned Australian history in my heart (the formalities took a little longer) in the fifth grade of primary school. To that point 'Australian History' comprised a doleful catalogue of self-styled 'explorers' who wandered in what large Mrs O'Loughlin used to call 'dretful desarts' glumly littering names about—Mount Disappointment, Mount Despair, Mount Hopeless—until, thankfully, they 'perished'. (Even in those benighted days I noticed that during their wanderings they would occasionally totter past people called Aborigines, and I would think 'at least somebody knows how to manage out there'.) I would look at the wavery little tracks the feckless white fellows had left on the school-reader map, and know I wanted nothing to do with them, or any who came after them.

For over thirty years as a professional historian living and working in this country I avoided our history. I know the Australia of the past as I know Chekhov's or Tolstoy's or Nabokov's Russia: from novels. Like my Russia, my Australia floats somewhere beyond historical time and geographical actuality. It is a bleached valley, a cluster of tall rooms embraced by a verandah; a suburb; a style, a set of possibilities.

Or so it was. After my transplant and for no clear reason I can fathom, but perhaps a desire for a wider, more stable context, I wanted to learn more. Another round of novels? Biographies, perhaps? No: I wanted direct access. I would do what historians always do; I would go to the sources. Or, rather, to one source: this was to be a Sunday stroll, not a major expedition with elephants and guns. And I wanted at least the illusion of serendipity. I wanted my source somehow to come to me, to appear, like a note in a bottle, a message from another time tossed to land at my feet.

And so it happened. Pursuing a quite different matter, I came upon a couple of paragraphs written by a Mr G. A. Robinson. I already knew something of Robinson: that he had been Protector of the Aborigines in Tasmania in the early days, that he had been somehow mixed up with Truganini, the 'last of the Tasmanian Aborigines', that he had brought her to Victoria. That he affected a strange cap, like a pastrycook gone to sea. And that he was a foolish and arrogant man, or was I mixing him up with someone else?

I asked an Australianist busy consulting me as a historical document if he had any of Robinson's writings. He had: Robinson's journal of a five-month-long horseback journey made during the winter of 1841 from Melbourne to Portland and back, with a swing through the Grampians on the home leg. In 1839, after Tasmania, he had been appointed Chief Protector of the Aborigines for Port Phillip District. He was to make over twenty similar expeditions through his new territories, keeping journals throughout. The one my friend handed to me had been edited by an ex-student of ours named Gary Presland, and published by the Victorian Archaeological Survey. Did I want more? Did I want a full bibliography?

I did not. The transplant had murdered patience. I had my note in a bottle. I would uncork the bottle and release the Mr Robinson held inside. I would get to know him, and he would be my guide. Of course there were other Mr Robinsons: in the memories of those who had known him; lurking in libraries in the pages of novels and histories. There were the Mr Robinsons of all those other journals; men of the same name and much the same body, but differently freighted by experience and expectation. It was the

Mr Robinson revealed between 20 March and 15 August 1841 that I was after.

For a historian it is luxurious indulgence to settle to a single, circumscribed text. Private journals can be expansive, unbuttoned affairs and, if regularly kept, hold at least the promise of revealing not only 'character', but the natural movement of the writer's mind. A couple of hours reading and I knew I was in luck. Mr Robinson was a most devoted journal-keeper.

Almost every night, whatever the hardships of the day, and after he has talked with any 'sable friends' about, he secludes himself to write. The white men travelling with him are convicts or servants: he neither desires nor brooks any intimacy with them. He has his journal for company. His tone slides easily from the practical to something very like the conjugal. He might begin with the weather, and a sharp, analytic account of terrain traversed. There might be housekeeping to do: out-goings of potatoes, blankets, shirts; incomings of natives contacted. He jots down words to add to his lists, of places seen and persons met with, of plants, animals, tools. He relaxes, remembering beguiling things—a flight of blue parrots, a genial dog, geese thick as waterlilies on a reedy lake. (He notices animals, and is tender towards them.) And he rehearses the events of the day: confides conversations and encounters, shapes them into narratives, sets them down. His journal will serve as a source for official reports, but it is very much more than that: it is a reviewing, a refreshment, a re-creation of his most private self. He and his journal, in whatever frail light, on those wintry nights, in those comfortless camps.

And we, you and I, reading over his shoulder. Against the odds, the Chief Protector is a natural writer. Occasionally he strikes a conventional attitude, or a too-laconic note stares mutely, but typically he is as direct and crisp as his weather reports: 'Severe frost during the night, ice this morning near thick as a dollar. Fine sunny day, tranquil light air.' He wastes little ink on men's appearances—it is character he cares about—but he can toss off the memorable vignette, as of his deplorable convict servant Myatt, negligently negotiating 'the van' through a pass, 'chanting over a doleful ditty peculiar to his class...his hat over his eyes as he generally wore it...occasionally run[ning] against stumps and then damning the horses for not taking care'. Arrived at Portland town, Robinson is dined, with metropolitan formality, by Commissioner Tyers. The rest of the company is 'a Mr Primrose, who fills a plurality of offices here as clerk to the bench, sub-collector of customs, and post master. He wears moustaches, and rings on each finger, is tall with a morose countenance,' and there stands Mr Primrose the rusticated dandy, waiting for Chekhov. Robinson's drawings speckling his text are equally vivid: they are as awkward, serious and expressive as a child's. Every cross-hatch of a net, every rail of a fence, is firmly inked in. An Aboriginal girl peacocking in a European frock vibrates with delight; an Aboriginal dancer hooded with grass explodes from spindly legs.

Mr Robinson quickly proves his worth as a guide. He links me back to places long known, but known in the flat, two-dimensional way of places called into being by one's arrival and dissolving on departure: places without a known past. On a still autumn day near

Port Campbell many years ago I watched my young sons dive for sea treasure. Crusts of blue pottery glinted in their hands. More sea treasure: in the April of 1841 'a large quantity of wax candles' drifts ashore on a nearby beach. Local blacks tie the candles in their hair; local whites trade in them. The price rockets: Mr Robinson is gratified to be given 'three or four'. For years I have felt a subliminal twitch of irritation when I cross a bridge on the way to our Anglesea beach house, thirty kilometres and half a lifetime away from my childhood beach house further down the coast. 'Merrijig Creek', the sign says, too sweetly. But Mr Robinson tells me *Merrijig* means 'good' or 'fine' in the local tongue: 'They asked me if I was pleased, saying Merrigic Elengermat, Merrigic Warr Nerbul, of course I say merrigic, and they were pleased.' Now I hear a babble of happy voices when I pass. Trivial things, but they render time transparent. A small new fact, and a landscape dulled by familiarity is suddenly sharp and clear; the details disaggregate, rearrange themselves, perspectives steady—and open like flowers. The past is present again: contingent, heavy with promise.

Or with shame. Elsewhere Robinson encounters a wandering family: a man, his wife, an infant, two very young girls. They are Wol-lore-rer, or what is left of them; the tribe, they say, is 'plenty all gone', 'plenty shoot him white man'. Robinson suspects that the little family is allowed to survive because the girls are kept at the 'nefarious disposal of white men'. His suspicions are confirmed when he hears them saying over their few words of English: 'Well done fuckumoll, go it fuckmoll, good night fuckmoll.'

'Wol-lore-rer.' A flinch of recognition: I knew a place called

Willaura, a small town between Ararat and Hamilton. I spent a few school holidays close by an even smaller place called Stavely. There were no people around then; just the scatter of big sheds and the little weatherboard house with the Harbells' place somewhere across the railroad track and over the rise. Nobody else. Just sheep, a few crows, the usual rabbits. Now there will always be people there: a man, his wife, a baby, and two little girls telling over the white man's litany: 'Well done fuckumoll. Go it fuckmoll. Good night fuckmoll.' And behind them, others. How many others?

Mr Robinson is a fine guide, to things unknown, or unacknowledged. He is also, it must be admitted, a rather foolish man. He lacks political sense, inflaming resentment in men on whom he must depend; he bullies and badgers subordinates, and bores and irritates superiors. Easily flattered, he is even more easily offended. He is impatient: he is always 'going on ahead' and getting lost, and when he does he blames someone else. He is humourless, priggish, jealous and vain.

He is also brave, independent and tough. He is making this journey, like most of his journeys, by choice. As Chief Protector he could have left the 'fieldwork'—the noting of past traces and present signs of Aboriginal presence, the listing of Aboriginal names of persons and places, the 'protection' of Aboriginal survivors—to his four assistants, who would have much preferred him to stay at home. But off he jogs in 1841 in his fifty-first year, a portly, high-coloured person. He rides with a leaf between his lips to protect them from sunburn, ranging up to fifty kilometres a day with the van dawdling along somewhere behind, subsisting largely on flour and tea and mutton—when he can get it, when Myatt hasn't lent the tinder box to a crony or forgotten to make the damper, when he hasn't got himself lost and has to spend the night hungry and huddled under a tree. Physically tough, his moral toughness is almost excessive: he advances on homesteads where he knows he will be less than welcome, where he must depend on the settler's hospitality; we tremble; in he stalks, stiff-necked, looking for trouble.

These are desperate times. Violence among blacks is increasing, between and within tribes, even within families, but it is violence between blacks and whites that he dreads. Rumours flicker ahead like marsh-fire: they must be tracked down and scotched, or many blacks might die. He can seem absurdly partisan. Whatever the fall of the evidence, he favours the natives. If sheep are missing, wild dogs did it, or the shepherds let them stray or exchanged them for access to a black woman. A shepherd speared through the walls of his hut as he sleeps must have provoked the attack. He believes such men, 'the sweepings of New South Wales and Van Diemen's Land', to be capable of anything. If their gentlemen employers might have little stomach for casual killings, they also know the value of sheep hauled stiff and seasick from the bowels of ships, or walked overland from Sydney. They are much too valuable to fetch up filling a native's shrunken belly. It is difficult to identify the shadows fleeing from the sheepfolds, difficult to identify them among the stringy figures down at the river camp. Best be rid of the lot: clear them off and keep them off, and if you have to use a few bullets to do it—well, so be it.

Robinson can see, in the silence of deserted habitations, in the faces of the frightened survivors, how close the settlers are to success. The signs are everywhere. At one of the few stations where blacks are still tolerated, a large swivel gun stands mounted at the homestead. Travelling through a specially tense region he makes only one entry for the day, but that is enough: 'All the shepherds I saw today have double barrel guns. The natives say, "by and by no good".'

The facts of white violence are easily discovered: the natives tell him. Their stories have the surreal authenticity of a silent film. At a camp near the Wannon in the Western District the people are weeping. A man and two women have been shot. 'The men had told them to come and they would give them damper. When they went, they shot them.' The little figures run, jerk, throw up their hands, fall. Who are the killers? 'Purbrick's men.' Their names? 'Jem, Barry and Bill or Paddy Jem and Bill or Bob and Larry...' The names are fluid as water. Robinson perseveres. He tracks the accused men down, and takes their statements. But he knows that nothing can come of it: with native testimony inadmissible in the courts, 'the whole matter falls to the ground, and the white ruffian may with impunity deny his black victim'.

Even when the killings are admitted there is no redress. Pyrenees natives give him the names of seven blacks shot by a leaseholder called Francis. Robinson records the names. Some days later he visits Francis at his homestead. The settler tells his story: he was riding down by the creek, natives attacked him, he shot four. He caught a black at his fold, and shot him, too. He had reported the incidents to the government. That, he assumes, will be the end of the matter.

As it proves. Robinson steps aside. 'I told [Francis] I did not intend to inquire, it was in [Assistant Protector] Parker's hands and was his duty.' Then he seems to forget the whole miserable business. Later that night he is deep in his domestic war with Myatt: the dolt has failed to shield the van against the weather, failed to make up his bed; he has had to do it himself; the rain beats in on him all night. But the killings are not forgotten. Francis had offered him a bed—a warm, dry bed, with 'clean sheets and pillowcases'. He had been insistent. He had even promised to play his fiddle—Francis is a lonely man. Robinson refuses: he will not be beholden to such a man. For the first time we hear what will become a little refrain: 'He acknowledged to five. The natives say seven.' Robinson goes back to his camp and his rain-wet bed, and writes it all down. Even if the law—the law whose agent he is—averts its face, he will keep the record. 'He acknowledged to five. The natives say seven.'

The evidence for some black crimes cannot be talked away. Robinson meets Governor La Trobe in Portland. La Trobe warns him not to take a newly contacted band of 'wild' natives too near the town. There has been a 'horrible murder' by Glenelg natives of a Mr Morton, a 'kind and humane gentleman', and his man Larry. The servant had been stretched on his back with spears driven through the palms of his hands, and 'they had cut the flesh off his bone when alive and eaten it'. They had also eaten of Morton's dead flesh. Robinson is shaken: he typically dismisses tales of cannibalism as hysterical fantasy ('all fudge!'), but he cannot impeach this source.

Later the same morning he is shepherding his 'shy and savage' flock to a more secure camping ground when they are hallooed after by a mob of predatory whalers, promising blankets, tomahawks, handkerchiefs, avid to get their hands on the Aboriginal women. He chivvies his people along, gets them settled. At midday Mr Blair, police magistrate at Portland, and Mr Henty, its leading citizen, seek him out at the camp. He records the ensuing conversation energetically, and at length. They being too mistrustful of the blacks to dismount, he must have had to look up at them throughout, which cannot have helped his temper. They show him the letter telling the gruesome details of the Morton killings. The two men 'were under great excitement—thought the natives of this [Glenelg] tribe should be exterminated'. Robinson admits his own dejection of spirit, but pleads the necessity of more knowledge, and more understanding. The discussion becomes warm. 'Mr Blair said he knew what he would do if he was Governor. He would send down soldiers and if they did not deliver up the murderer he would shoot the whole tribe. I said it would not perhaps be so easy. Mr Henty said there would be no difficulty on the Glenelg as they had only the river to fly to and they could soon flush them out from among the rocks.' And so, heatedly, on. Two days earlier Robinson had been desperate for these gentlemen's approbation, but when they finally turn their horses' heads for town he is heartily glad to be rid of them.

It is a taxing night. Both his own and the 'wild' people are in an excitable state. In a squabble over a piece of bread one of his men hurls a spear, which whizzes close by his head. More blacks arrive, strangers, 'the most turbulent and noisy natives' he has ever encountered. They settle themselves close by his tent. Sleep is impossible. Nonetheless, the old energy is back, and he is himself again. Alienated from his own people, surrounded by unknown, possibly dangerous natives, he is precisely where he chooses to be.

It is that steady preference which makes him remarkable. Irascible with whites, he is preternaturally patient with Aborigines. He is, in fact, a most earnest anthropologist. On Saturday 17 April he writes from Assistant Protector Sievwright's camp: '8 a.m. Heavy rain and a westerly wind…Busy collecting vocabulary. My tent, as usual, since day dawn thronged with natives.' This could be an extract from the great Malinowski's diary—except that Malinowski would never tolerate 'savages' in his tent. Robinson aims to record the name, land and family affiliations of every Aborigine he encounters. They yield their whitefellow names readily enough, but are reticent about their own. He coaxes them, carefully recording the strings of unfamiliar syllables. The driving, eye-baffling hand slows to careful legibility here. Talking with one group, he suspects a connection with a tribe to the east. He begins to pronounce the easterners' names. No response. He perseveres. 'Ning.cal.ler.bel.' The natives begin to sing. It is a long song, and 'at the end of each stanza Ning.cal.ler.bel was mentioned by name'. Bravo, Mr Robinson!

Yet he has the grace to acknowledge that even hard-won 'knowledge' can be wrong: he tirelessly checks his information. He is alert to the rhetorical element in native violence. When a melee erupts at Sievwright's camp—the men 'in single combat and then all together clubbing and wrestling', the women 'vociferating at the top of their breath'—all is ferocity and pandemonium. Yet, he notes, with interesting intermissions: 'at intervals the fighting would cease and the combatants would stop and taunt. A boomerang or spear would be thrown to provoke the combat and the battle renewed.' 'It reminded me,' Robinson writes, with uncharacteristic dryness, 'of a Hibernian fracas.'

He accepts close physical contact, and its penalties. 'Wild' Aborigines 'paw…me about', one in particular 'rubbing his hand about me…feeling my limbs and soliciting my clothes.' Vigorous investigation of his person escalates to what looks like a collective attempt at a shakedown: hands tug at his clothes, pull at his reins, slap at his horse; he retains his physical and moral poise. And when he contracts a painful and obstinate 'pustulence [sic] irruption' (scabies?) from those patting, poking hands he continues to offer up his person, saying: 'I could not rightfully be cross or unkind to these people. It was their custom and, as the old saying is, when in Rome do as Rome does.'

There is vanity in this. He enjoys the accoutrements of office: travelling heroically light, he nevertheless carts his Chief Protector's uniform with him, and wears it on grand occasions. And he loves being recognised. Riding ahead of his party, he comes upon women and children gathering yams. Normally they would scatter at the sight of a white man. 'When they saw me they ran to where I was standing. Joy was in their countenances.' He is even more delighted when a recognition scene is witnessed. Proceeding with his natives, a convict, and, by most happy chance, a local settler, Mr Adams, they see a long file of 'wild' natives, most of them armed, advancing towards them. 'The spears…were newly sharpened,' he says with relish, and we wonder how he knows.

Undaunted, alone, Robinson goes forward to meet them. 'I held up my hands.' They halt. Working his way down the line, 'I shook each of them by the hand and patted them on the head.' Their submission is immediate, total, glorious: 'They repeated every word I spoke to them…I distributed to each a medal which I suspended to their neck…' Gifts cascade from his hands: headbands, handkerchiefs, necklaces to the children. And then the punch line: 'Mr Adams said he never saw natives so obedient to anyone as those natives were to me.'

Mr Robinson's cup runneth over. That night he has a sack of Mr Adams's potatoes sent to the natives, and throws in a piece of pork for VDL Jack, his trusted Tasmanian assistant, and the reprobate Myatt. On the evening before a planned rendezvous with all the blacks of the Port Fairy region he is blissful: 'My mind is now at ease and I feel satisfied. Providence has crowned my endeavours with success.' The next day he crows, 'Such a meeting has never been held with these people, either within or out of their district…What has been done in 7 weeks!'

There are equally rapturous accounts of the trust he inspires in individuals. One example:

> I started from Synnott's with the Barcondeet native to give me information but as it was raining hard I cantered on at a brisk pace and my Aboriginal friend ran and kept pace with me. He was armed with spears. He kept chatting about his country and calling out the names of different locations and said his country was good country. I answered in the affirmation [sic] which afforded him satisfaction. I am certain the poor fellow

would have run the whole way, 12 miles, had I not stopped him and desired him to wait for the van and come with it.

It is an affecting picture: the young black rendered immune to rain and natural fatigue by affection, chattering freely in the benign presence of his Protector. Who, taking thought for his charge, gently puts an end to this enchanted run at the stirrup. We splutter and choke: Robinson glows. On that day of triumph near Port Fairy he had gone to the assembly point early, and had addressed no more than a few words to the nervous crowd when his entourage rolled in. Immediately, one old man 'thrust his arm in mine as if apprehensive of danger…and walked with me whilst I gave the necessary directions to my people'. Later, distributing gifts, 'I became most popular with the juveniles, even the little children came and clung onto my knees like children do a papa.'

Mr Robinson is getting a lot in return for those potatoes and headbands and handkerchiefs. Can a balance be drawn? To begin at the material level, it is painfully clear that the natives are hungry; that food is the most urgent necessity. Robinson keeps an anxious watch on the depletion of native game, but the vestigial groups he and we encounter could not hunt anyway, and their vegetable foods were being ravaged by imported flocks. He does what he can, coaxing and bullying flour or sugar or the occasional wether out of grudging settlers, but it is never enough: even the feeding of his immediate entourage reads like a continuous loaves-and-fishes miracle. Knowing the bitter cold of southern nights, he hands out blankets when he has them, but blankets are in short supply. For the rest, he might barter a knife for a spear, or reward a special courtesy with a tomahawk, but what he mainly gives are small, cheap, easily transportable things: caps, beads, medals, and lots of cards, or 'letters', as he sometimes calls them, magnificently inscribed with his own or the Governor's name.

At a casual glance this looks to be the familiar swindle: the European trash deployed in a thousand shameful encounters to bamboozle and diddle the locals. Certainly Robinson seems blind to the gulf in utility between the objects he offers for those he covets for his 'collection': a cap for a cherished spear or a woman's indispensable bark bucket is no exchange. Perhaps there can be no equitable exchange between a people with an abundance of mass-produced items, some of them purely decorative, and another whose economy is so dour that bodies are rendered sacred by the application of mud. But the flow of small, highly visible objects has less to do with exchange than with power. To Mr Robinson, they signify personal authority. To other whites they offer reassurance: a warrior sporting a cap and clutching the Governor's card seems no longer a warrior. There is, however, another effect. A native in a cap holding out his card or his medal can be less easily classified as a natural but undesirable infestation of the land: he is marked, however feebly, as human, and so, potentially, within the protection of the law.

There is a kind of reciprocity here, if a skewed and fragile one. But the limits are firmly drawn. Coming upon some shelters, Robinson and his party prowl about, and pry into the baskets they find hidden in a couple of hollow trees. Robinson acknowledges some feelings of delicacy—he looks, he says, only because 'the customs and manners of these people were new to me'—but he looks nonetheless. He finds a jumble of objects: bone awls; bits of broken glass, of lava, of scoria; lumps of ochre and pipeclay and iron; a stick for stripping bark; an amulet; a few items of European dress.

It is a poignant collection, this survival kit for difficult times, and we can only guess at its meaning. Robinson takes two of the awls, leaving 'a new cotton handkerchief' in return. He takes something else, and for this he leaves no payment: 'I found a lead pencil whole in their basket and as I needed it, I took it away.' He does not wonder how they got the pencil, or why they treasure it. The instruments of literacy belong to him.

On the emotional plane the scales tilt differently. Robinson is a good anthropologist because he is attentive to his subjects' behaviour, and he is attentive because they charm him. For a time I was puzzled by his inattention towards his most familiar black companion, 'VDL Jack'. He had brought Jack with him from Tasmania, along with Truganini and fourteen others, as 'personal attendants', but he also called them his family. The Governor felt himself duped, and complained at the expense.

Jack—alias Tunerminnerwait or Napoleon—and four more of Robinson's Tasmanians, three of them women, one of them Truganini, were to become suddenly, shockingly famous as black insurrectionists late in 1841, when they carried out a series of raids and robberies around Point Nepean—robberies in which two whalers were killed. Desperation had a lot to do with it, their rations having been stopped by the frugal La Trobe. Jack would be hanged for murder in January 1842. At this stage, half a year before, he is indispensable: he guards the camp, finds lost wagons and horses, and informs on black and white alike. And when Robinson wearies of the all-too-carnal investigations of curious 'friends', he hands Jack over to them like an amiable long-limbed doll. Yet Robinson's references to him are few, and coolly instrumental. I suspect it is Jack's sophistication, his learnt amenability, which has rendered him uninteresting in his master's eyes. Robinson is quickly wearied by excessively 'wild' natives, with whom he can have no 'intelligent conversation'. He is bored by docile ones, save as stock figures for the *tableaux-vivant* of his private theatre of vanity. What he likes are people sufficiently knowledgeable of white men's ways to be attentive, yet who retain their exuberance and spontaneity.

Consider his attitude to Eurodap, alias 'big' Tom Brown, who makes his entry into the journal on 6 April 1841. Initially he is allocated three characteristics: 'This was an intelligent man,' 'he had on a jacket and trousers,' '[he] was quite delighted to see me.' Thenceforth Eurodap slips constantly in and out of the pages. He is useful: he knows the country, he supplies names for places and things, and when strange natives are sighted it is Eurodap who is sent out to fetch them in. But Eurodap is primarily valued not for his usefulness, but for his personality: his vivacity, his expressivity, his gaiety. When new groups must be entertained with song, Eurodap excels. He takes joyful liberties. Robinson detests obscenities, especially in native mouths. 'Fudge!' is his own most violent epithet. So Eurodap plays Grandmother's Steps with irascible Robinson: 'Eurodap said white shepherd too much no good talk to black fellow and then gave me a specimen of his proficiency etc. g-d d-m, you bl—y lyer; you old bugger; be off; d-mn you, etc., etc. He was going on with these blasphemous epithets when I told him to desist and that they were very bad.'

Then comes the journal entry for 25 June. It comprises two sentences: 'Tom Brown killed. Went from McRae's to Winter's.' The entry following briefly describes Eurodap's death: he has been speared in some fracas, seemingly while trying to mediate. And the journal's sturdy march through the days collapses. It is impossible to establish clear detail or sequence: there are seven separate entries, all of them confusingly dated, for the four days following the death. Only on 29 June does the steady progression re-assert itself.

Am I making too much of this break in what seems to be a pattern? Perhaps. Were this fiction, I would know that all things said and left unsaid, all disruptions, were intended to signify. But this is not fiction, and I cannot be sure. I do know that Robinson, among whites a stiff, awkward fellow, and tensely competitive, is with Eurodap and others like him relaxed and genial, because he need fear no challenge. With them he believes he finds the security of uncontested because uncontestable inequality. In their company, and possibly only in their company, can his human affections be fully liberated.

This is, perhaps, 'condescension' in the old sense, of affability towards one's putative inferiors. But it is also something very like love. While most whites view the exuberance of black sociability with distaste shading into revulsion, Robinson basks in it. Blacks swarm in and out of his tent without let or hindrance. Information sessions are informal to unruliness: he grumpily complains of the impossibility of getting everything down on paper when two or three people are simultaneously roaring out the names of creatures they have collected for him. He attends corroborees eagerly, and stays to the end. When the going is hard he walks so that blacks may ride—'to encourage them,' he says. He persuades nervous novices to climb on his horse, and laughs at the result. And he responds with expeditious tenderness to individual distress. An old chief he had talked with through a long evening is embroiled in what becomes 'a general fight with clubs and mulgas' at Sievwright's camp, a fight which Robinson implies he quells: 'I went among them.' The old man, wounded, excited, urges the whites to get their guns and shoot the opposition. Robinson coaxes him into the assistant protector's hut, and soothes him with tea and damper, and later he orders a general feast of 'mutton, potatoes and tea' for all combatants. I have become very fond of Mr Robinson.

Robinson also actively enjoys physical contact with bodies other whites see as diseased, verminous, loathsome. 'Pustulent irritations' notwithstanding, if he is hugged, he hugs back. On no direct evidence whatsoever I am confident that he shares his blanket from time to time with one of the 'fine, sprightly girls' he admires so frankly. He accepts other gifts freely offered, he is susceptible to women, so why not? ('When in Rome...') It is the brutal sexual politics of most black–white couplings which appals him, not the sexual act.

Of course he does not really 'do as in Rome'. The assumption of special status is always there. He records the native protocols governing encounters between strangers—the period of silent watchfulness, identification through the painting of faces and bodies, the formal exchange first of words, then of song and dance—but he does not follow them. On the contrary, 'when natives appear I break through all Aboriginal ceremony…and go forth and meet them'. Once again we hear that biblical reverberation. But I doubt his physical tolerance and ready emotional intimacy finds its ground in some bloated messianic fantasy. His relaxation and warmth of spirit before Aboriginal otherness is a private, secular grace.

The traffic is not entirely one way. A recurrent anguish in the study of cross-cultural communications is to watch questions being asked from one side which can make no sense at all to the other. Across the gulfs of time we hear the silence of perfect incomprehension. But Mr Robinson asks the right questions. This is an accident: his purpose is to collect things, above all names, of individuals, clans, places, and he is eager to get the affiliations right. Fortuitously, what the blacks take him to be doing is mapping the Aboriginal world of meanings and imagination.

That makes him a man worth talking to—a man to whom it is possible to talk, who will understand. Just west of Mount Cole he falls in with several families. 'I repeated a string of names of tribes and localities all of which they knew, and were astonished at the extent of my information.' He so impresses another woman with his knowledge of 'tribes and persons and localities' that she is persuaded that he must have been a native of those parts come back as a white, and grills him until she has constructed a plausible genealogy for him. An old woman, wandering with the remnants of her family over their usurped land, responds to his questions when they have lit a fire and sat down around it. She 'enacts a variety of events connected with the history of her country', and then, 'in a dejected and altered tone', deplores its loss.

Robinson interprets all such eagerness to talk with him as naive tributes to his personal charisma. He does not ask why the magic works best on blacks who have already experienced white depredations. What we must remember is that Robinson presents himself as a man of authority, claiming access to remote powers. He also inquires into serious Aboriginal matters. And then he writes such matters down (remember the pencil). I suspect it is this rather than his personal allure which makes Aborigines ready, even desperate, to talk with him.

He is also a man capable of astonishing, painful complacency. A few days before the end of his journey, when he draws nearer to Melbourne, a handful of natives, survivors from two tribes, attach themselves to him. He notes that they are 'very communicative'. They are also eager for connection: they give him a new name, 'meaning in their own tongue "great" or "big" chief'. They beg his protection against the whites, who 'drove them away and said be off'. 'Too much "be off" all about,' they say.

Robinson tells them he might help them later, but that he has no time now. They weep and ask him for a 'letter' and, when he leaves, their leader pursues him to offer a last-minute gift: a particularly fine emu-feather belt. Surely they are desperate for his intervention? Surely he can smell their fear? We can: the pages reek with it.

It seems, however, that he cannot. He remarks on the intelligence of one of the young men ('a promising youth if attended to') as if we were still at the dawn of the world. Then, charmed with his new name, delighted with his gift—flattered by the tears—he rides cheerfully on. He finds the day 'beautiful', the country 'uncommonly good and pleasant'. He concludes the entry with a casual observation: 'These plains must ultimately be made use of for sheep grazing. The government must lease them.'

Sir Thomas More summed up the human agony attending the great land-grabs of sixteenth-century England in a masterly image: 'Your sheep, that were wont to be so meek and tame, and so small eaters, now...be become so great devourers, and so wild...that they eat up and swallow down the very men themselves.' Three centuries later, we watch that perversion in nature being re-enacted in an English colony. Two peoples whose interests are perfectly inimical are in contention for the land. The Aboriginals are the weaker; they will go to the wall. Astonishingly, no provision is made for them: they are cast out of their territories to die. That much is cruelly apparent from Robinson's own writings. So how to explain that casual, shocking comment? What is wrong with this man? Is he a fool, a hypocrite, a moral imbecile; another thick-skinned imperialist playing bumpo with a wincing world?

I think he is none of those things. Rather, he, like so many others, has contrived ways to live with the appalling, immutable fact of Aboriginal death. Initially, his brisk tone, his lack of introspection, his radiant vanity, led me to think him a straightforward sort of chap.

That was, as it always is, hubris: 'simplicity' in humans is a reflex of distance. How many of us dare to pretend to understand those to whom we stand closest, and how great the punishment of those who do.

I have come to think that Robinson lives in the stretch of a terrible contradiction, the tension of the stretch being betrayed in persistent patterns of conduct—for example, that compulsive 'going on ahead'—and equally persistently, if more subtly, in certain oddities of style. As I read, I was more and more struck by disjunctions not adequately explained by appeal to the 'journal format': too-abrupt transitions between subjects, irritable returns to matters done with, radical switches of mood. An unmoored sentence recalls some past contretemps. The affair bites at him still. He rails for a sentence or a paragraph against 'the condition of the original inhabitants of this land'—then pivots abruptly back into busywork.

These disjunctions thicken at times of tension. It is as if his mind suddenly lurches, and swerves from some unseen impediment. I have come to think that these judderings, along with his irritable, urgent energy, are indicators of what we used to call 'cognitive dissonance': an uncomfortable condition in which a mind veers and twists as it strives to navigate between essential but mutually incompatible beliefs. Time and again he approaches overt acknowledgment of the incorrigibility of black–white relations; time and again he pulls away to the refuge of the trivial and merely vexing.

He 'believes' in his work: that is transparently clear. But he also knows, at some level, if only intermittently, that his naggings about the law and his handing out of blankets and letters are futile; that he can do nothing to slow the avalanche. His treasured authority gives him power to coerce only the victims, not their oppressors. 'I sent for this native but the man said he would not come. I said he was under my protection and I would soon make him.' The equations are bleak. The law is the blacks' only protection: the law grants away their lands, and fails to protect them from wanton, most deliberate murder. The Chief Protector, for all his posturings and protestations, can effect nothing. The Chief Protector is a sham.

These are unendurable truths. So he keeps himself busy: he quibbles and quarrels and shifts the blame, lectures stiff-faced settlers, pats the patting black hands, hands out his blankets and his cards. He is hopelessly divided: scanning the land for kangaroos, he is simultaneously assessing its potential as pasture. He indulges in the fantasy of missionaries everywhere: somehow, the natives must be quarantined from the contagion of evil. 'White men of respectable character', men like himself, should 'attach themselves to the native tribes and control their movements.' But even if that were to happen (he knows it will never happen) where could they go? He strives to gather up his wandering people like some Old Testament prophet in flight from catastrophe. But the catastrophe is all around him, and there is no Promised Land.

So on he rides, watching for signs: a curl of smoke, boughs bent to shelter shivering bodies. He is searching for ghosts and the shadows of ghosts. He sees crumbling mounds of shells or the long depressions which mark communal ovens, and hears the silent hubbub of a vanished encampment. He gathers up the survivors, distributes his little gifts, lights his illusory flares of hope. He counts his flock, scrupulously; he records their names. Absurdly, he gives them new ones, but these are not real names. Real names differentiate and connect; they have social meaning. These names, like his medals and his letters and his blankets, are tokens merely: amulets against death. These people are ghosts already, they have no substance. At a station one day, begging flour, they are gone the next. They can be made to vanish at a word: 'He said he would have none of them about his station.' 'Be off!' These Joes and Jacks and Mollys have entered the numbered anonymity of death: 'He acknowledged to five. The natives say seven.'

Every night this burdened, driven man steals time from sleep to assemble his information, to fix the flux of experience, to construct his self-protective, self-exposing account of things. He is an addicted writer. Some entries—those triumphalist narratives and tableaux, with their preposterous biblical resonances—must have been long in the writing. He has taken pleasure in their crafting. And occasionally, just occasionally, especially when he has been forced to stare for a moment into the abyss between rhetoric and action, he stumbles upon images of haunting power.

From the first days of his journey he makes frequent reference to a place called Boloke. There is a lake there, and an abundance of fish and fowl which still draws natives from all over the region. So rich is the abundance that this is a traditional meeting-place for the ceremonial resolution of conflict, a place of feasting and of celebration. Through the slow drudge of days Boloke shimmers on the edge of awareness as a vision of peace and plenty. Then he goes there—to find desolation. The lake waters have been sucked up by drought. There are signs of many natives: 'a vast number' of old shelters, abandoned tools, and everywhere on the beach their tracks, 'thick as sheep tracks'. On this day he sees not one. Instead there are dead eels, on the sand, on the banks, strewed along the beach. At the deserted camps 'dead eels lay in mounds; thousands of dead eels, and very large ones too'. Crows are feasting upon them. There are also 'numerous tracks of cattle, sheep and horses'.

Robinson lingers: he looks, wonders, notes down what he sees. Then he moves on to more practical matters—but not before he has fixed an image which murmurs awareness of that other, invisible, more terrible destruction. Later, visiting the Francis homestead, he flounders, making his only protest against the settler's self-admitted slaughter of blacks by refusing a bed for the night, even when an Aboriginal eyewitness confirms his suspicion that Francis and his men had killed the people down at the river camp without provocation. Robinson keeps his miserable peace.

Then, as he mounts his horse to leave the following day, he sees a human skull. He has seen skulls on display often enough, nailed to doors and posts in particularly troubled areas, but this one is lying on open ground, a few metres from the woolshed and hard by the road, 'on a small bare hill where sheep had been folded'. Robinson realises that it must be the skull of the man Francis had shot at the sheepfold; that he had ordered that the body be left to lie where it fell. 'I showed it to the natives and they said "Mr Francis killed him, Mr Francis shot plenty blackfellows, all gone black fellows." "What had happened to the rest of the body?" "Taken away by the dogs." '

Robinson picks up the skull, puts it in his van. And then he continues with his travels and his general observations: 'Francis is fencing in a paddock; he has a woolshed and several huts. The soil in this part of the country is of an inferior quality, red sandy loam from 2 to 3 inches deep...'

From horror to banality in a breath. Nonetheless, the horror is preserved, and now it is there in the record, for any of us to read.

Across a landscape transformed by our meeting I look back to Mr Robinson. He is riding through a cold rain. A figure runs beside him, running easily over the land. He is young, and strong, but he is already a ghost. Perhaps he knows that, because as he runs he names the places of this his country. Measuring his breath to his stride, he sings its names and its beauty. It is possible that this white man will hear, and hearing, write. It is possible that someone, some day, will read, and remember.

ON MEMORY: EEL OR CRYSTAL?

SNAPSHOTS

Writing Mr Robinson was my first piece of formal writing—writing designed for publication—after the transplant operation. There could have been no better therapy. I had become used to the solitary disciplines of convalescent invalidism: pill-taking, going-to-clinic, cautious exercise, resting. Now I had Mr Robinson for company. He revived the addictive pleasures of immersion in the situation, experiences and mind of a stranger dead long before I was born, with all these things lurking, waiting to be recovered, in the marks he had made on paper in life. That is the reliable miracle of history.

Mr Robinson also gave me a future. He made me aware that other tragic human histories had been masked by my own. As my strength slowly returned, I knew that, given time and breath, I would search those histories out.

And he gave me mind-baffling problems to untangle. He was so vital a presence because I was working from his journal, a document of immediate record free both from the artifices of conscious self-presentation and from the flamboyant vagaries of memory—vagaries I had recently learnt rather too much about. I knew I would have to think harder about the workings of memory, because it is on memory that the whole enterprise of history, along with the more anxious enterprise of sustaining a reasonably stable sense of self, depends.

I was also discovering that memory, especially the luminous fragments left over from childhood, can be the secret kindling for fiction.

Why do we want to remember childhood at all? For most of our adult years it seems a remote and empty time—the time before we turned into whatever and whoever we turned out to be. A few years further on, parents and siblings ignored for decades fill our dreams, along with forgotten cats and cousins and neighbourhood dogs. Childhood becomes our surest homeland: the time when we were unequivocally, sometimes rapturously, ourselves, unmarked by compromise and disappointment, undulled by drab maturity.

Most of the moments and places inhabiting my childhood memory are bathed not in Nabokovian gold but in the sepia melancholy of old photographs. I know this is the effect conventionally attached to such photographs, but in my case the melancholy is not, I think, a present imposition, but what I felt at the time. The shouts of my brothers playing cricket at Geelong's Queen's Park or ducking each other in the Barwon River seemed separated from me even as I was chasing the tennis balls, or dangling from the old landing stage with two metres of brown water and the slimy corpses of drowned sheep moving silently beneath me (I couldn't swim).

What I felt, had I known the word, was alienated. I knew I was in the picture but I also knew that was what it was: a picture. When we went down to the old ice house and shouted against the cliffs to hear the echo, the early clamour would recede to a single, quivering note, very pure, very distant. That was the sound I listened for, the sound which thrilled me, which matched my view of things, which seemed to me to comprehend the essence of existence.

While often melancholy, I was not at all unhappy. I doubt that phrases like 'a happy childhood', 'an unhappy childhood', mean much, unless there is deliberate abuse, beyond what they suggest about adult sentimentality. A child can suffer misery of a purity unknown in adult life, but that is a separate issue. I can remember being consciously happy on two occasions: once riding with Herbie and the baker back to school at lunchtime, and once, stretched on the back lawn, buffalo grass prickling my thighs, listening to the bees in the apple trees, gazing into the vanishing blue of a February sky, and languorously milking the chilled juice of an orange into my mouth. And thinking, as the juice trickled down my throat, 'Here, now, I am completely, utterly happy.'

Of course there were bad times. The worst ones no-one else in the household would have much noticed, like the sick helplessness of being labelled a liar. As a child I was a desperate, doomed liar when cornered. Now I am, on the whole, remarkably truthful, lying only with the finest calculation. I don't intend to suffer that humiliation again. I was always vulnerable to the Word. While I had to learn that sticks and stones could break your bones, I always knew that names could finish you for good. When you are a child, everyone feels free to call you names. And every name matters, because the world is your sole, unforgiving mirror.

What was reliably best about childhood—what I miss most now it is gone, what being in hospital gave back to me—was its spaciousness: the multiplicity of sensations to be extracted from the infinitudes of time inhabiting every day, the infinitude of spaces in even a modest house. In the oblong tent under the table, shielded by the tablecloth curtain and the palisade of familiar legs, at once in society and out of it; under the ironing board, hearing the hiss of the iron on sprinkled sheets, breathing the hot moist air with its inexplicable whiff of new bread; resting my chin on the edge of the mottled slab of marble where my mother mixed scones out of lard and flour, salt and water with a magician's aplomb. Crouched beside the sewing machine I confronted slavery long before I knew the term, as the black man built into my mother's Singer plunged and lunged in submission to her rocking foot. Squatting in the sawdust desert in the slatted light of under-the-house, a striped tea-towel on my head, I was in Arabia. A different tea-towel, and it was Africa.

Time was always there to be played with: made to vanish in sea dramas staged with press-ganged harlequin bugs, leaves and a bucket of water; prolonged by deliberately aimless wanderings; or stopped altogether through long afternoons, with even the kitten asleep.

Ours was a small house with six people in it, but my memories are of being alone: my mother in her bedroom, door shut, taking her interminable afternoon rest, my brothers out somewhere, everyone out somewhere—just me and the boundless fifteen by fifty metres of our block. In the silent hall in late afternoon, watching the dust motes dancing and the coloured lozenges from the leadlighted front door trembling on the wall, or drifting out to the beehive by the lemon tree to see the bees come home, I was pervaded with a luxurious sense of the evanescence—not knowing the word, but perfectly familiar with its sense—of all these arrangements: houses, families, people, creatures, things.

And also of their tenacity. There was an antiquated wind-up record player inside the hall cabinet, its one dusty record permanently on the spindle waiting to be cranked into life. I may have been forbidden to touch it. I know I approached it with beating heart. I would wind the handle, lower the needle, and a voice would come spindling out, a voice too old and frail to be male or female, but still ineffably human. It would sing: 'Carry me back to old Virginney, there's where the cotton and the corn and 'tatoes grow', the voice quivering, the sound attenuating, almost vanishing, but always, barely, audible, and I thought the voice had somehow been trapped back there in long-ago Virginney, a slave voice mourning in that alien place, and that I was briefly liberating it from the black bakelite to mourn and tremble in the afternoon stillness of a hall of a suburban house in Australia.

A childhood caught in a clutter of memory-snapshots. Did I do what any halfway respectable historian would do and consult my alternative source, my surviving sibling, to see how far our memories match? Three years older than I, he had been from my first awareness my enemy, reasonably enough, being the supplanted knee-baby. Now we are friends, the only people alive in the world who know how it was with us once.

But I did not question him. Private memories are both the products and the possessions of the private self. My brother's memories, like his experiences within our family household, are his. They will be quite unlike mine.

Besides, it would only make trouble. We are notoriously dismissive of other people's recollections, and ferocious in defence of our own. Friendships, marriages, families, whole societies have foundered on contended accounts of the past. The repertoire of shared stories families trade in has been fixed in the telling: converted into social currency, drained of their private meanings. Private memories are best kept private. Memories-become-anecdotes kill the moment quite as effectively as do photographs. Salman Rushdie has one of his protagonists say:

> I told you the truth…Memory's truth, because memory has its own special kind. It selects, eliminates, alters, exaggerates, minimises, glorifies, and vilifies also; but in the end it creates its own reality, its heterogeneous but usually coherent version of events; and no sane human being ever trusts someone else's version more than his own.

He is right on all counts. For all my training in scepticism, I cannot repudiate my memories, or even much refine them: mine, like yours, are simply there, as indubitable, as particular, as our feet.

And my brother could not know my dominant childhood mood, which was a most voluptuous melancholy. Despite the appearance of drift, I was never the least bored, because there was also, every day and always, my main and compelling activity: spying on my mother.

A hundred analysts of various persuasions agree that childhood matters. Indeed they tell us that by childhood's end everything that matters has already happened; that those empowered to read our nursery scripts will find our histories already indelibly inscribed there—histories that we poor fools are condemned to repeat until in pure exhaustion we die. And childhood, at least early childhood, is always about mother. She is the context and touchstone for all new experiences, the guarantor of all reiterated ones. Or was. In these days of conscientious co-parenting it may be that matters are different.

Most mothers in the simple world of fiction, excluding the genre of witch-mothers, symbolise security—warm breasts, milk, apple-cake, uncritical love. My mother didn't. Instead she provided me with an inspiriting mystery: the obdurate opacity of other beings. She also provided me with an absorbing occupation. I was determined to fathom her secret life.

She puzzled me from the beginning, or at least as soon as I knew us to be separate persons, which must have been very early. I have a wisp of memory of slowly subsiding sideways into her lap, presumably after the evening meal, and then the jerky movement of being carried, of chilly sheets, of footsteps going away. I remember being perched on the edge of the kitchen table, my brothers perched beside me, the floor dangerously far away, and having my face swiped with a sour-smelling flannel and my gritty knees scrubbed. These attentions felt more like assaults than affection, as they probably were, towards evening, when she had been working all day. She always knew her duty. When I began school she would stand me in front of her kitchen chair every night to twist my lank hair into rags tied so tight that my eyes turned Chinese and I could not lay my spiky head on the pillow, all so that I could take five skinny spirally curls to school, with a big green taffeta bow on top. Both of us knew she did this not for pride or vanity, but out of a kind of pity, because I was so grimly plain. In second grade I cut the curls off, crunch crunch, with the blunt scissors set out for craft, and after that she left me alone.

My obsession with my mother was surprising because there was another female in the family about whom I could have been expected to be more curious. My sister was thirteen years older than I. Despite sharing a room with her for much of my childhood, I knew her very little during those years, although later, when she was ill with the cancer which was to kill her, we came to love each other; to know what it was to be sisters.

In childhood my sister was an assemblage of parts: the stockings I washed, the silver dancing shoes I stroked to brightness, the light brown hair with golden glints I shampooed and rolled on Saturday mornings, the armfuls of net and tulle engulfing the kitchen table on Saturday afternoons. Together we concocted the radiant being who swept out of the house on Saturday nights to captivate local society at the Geelong Palais de Danse.

While I was passionately interested in her accoutrements, and eager to restore them to order when I would wake to find them scattered around our room on Sunday mornings—my sister a lump in her bed—I was never in the least curious about what she did when she was out of the house, presumably recognising that everything that mattered in her life was happening far beyond my territory.

What mystified me about my mother was that everything that happened to her happened and could only happen inside the house, where I was on guard, and where nothing ever happened. Therefore whatever was happening to her was happening somewhere else—somewhere concealed from direct observation. Somewhere hidden either in some other place, or somewhere within. So I became a full-time private investigator, with an ever-expanding repertoire of techniques.

I would interview her, usually in the washhouse on Monday mornings when she could be relied on to remain relatively stationary. At the time of these interrogations my head did not quite reach the edge of the concrete trough. How old would that make me? Five? Not yet at school, anyway. Nonetheless, I had a lot of topics to draw on because we listened to the ABC on the radio every day until the twelve o'clock news and lunch.

My technique was not good. I was always too eager. I always moved too fast. Who was her favourite singer? Paul Robeson. Her favourite song? 'The Open Road', sung by John Charles Thomas. Her favourite film star? Errol Flynn. Why did she like Errol Flynn? No answer. Did she like Errol Flynn better than…my father? A contemptuous glance—for the stupidity of the question? Because she so much preferred my father? Or because it was ridiculous to suggest that she liked him at all? Compressed lips, end of interview.

I studied her language, her turns of speech. I somehow knew

that when we'd ask her what was for tea and she'd say 'bread and pullet' or 'bread and duck-under-the-table' she was drawing on common stock, on generations of parents intent on keeping children down and in their proper place. But sometimes she would say mysterious, disturbing things. Things like: 'You're not as green as you're cabbage-looking.' She would say this with a reflective, measuring glance—really looking at me, and saying directly to me, 'You're not as green as you're cabbage-looking.' What could it mean? It baffled me for years. By about fourth grade I had turned it from an incomprehensible string of words into a parseable sentence. By fifth grade I was gratified to realise that it wasn't an insult, or at least not a direct one. Later still, after I had left home, it would float into my mind and I would laugh: at my own childish anxiety, at how much of my mother was that convoluted compliment, negated at the moment of its giving. Not absolutely green, but irretrievably cabbage-looking.

Then, years after that, I came across it in print, and a golden bubble of childhood collapsed into vague wetness. She had tricked me. These words which I had thought her personal coining, a communiqué addressed to me out of her unique being, were simply a quaint saying, a promiscuous proverb at home in everybody's mouth. She had evaded me again.

Every afternoon she would vanish into her bedroom, 'to read', she said. I didn't believe she read in there. For a long time I didn't believe that people read books at all. I was a backward reader, making no sense of the smudgy sticks and squiggles until deep into second grade. Looking at newspapers made sense because newspapers had pictures in them. But not books. I could not imagine what people were really up to when they held a book. Their faces went still, their eyelids nearly closed, and if I spoke to them they looked at me through eyes gone blank and unfocused.

At least my father 'read' in his chair in the dining room, where I could keep an eye on him, and after a few minutes he would go properly to sleep, and the mysterious pretence would be over. My mother would go into her room, and shut the door. But she kept her library books on the hall table, and when I finally got the knack of reading I would steal them one by one and consume them in rushed gobbets in the dead grey light of the dining room. I don't remember much about them, except *Tobacco Road*, written by someone called Erskine Caldwell. I was shocked by *Tobacco Road*, by those people who could hardly speak but who committed rape or incest or worse from dawn until dark and later. I did not want my mother reading that kind of stuff. I considered taking it down to the river and drowning it, but respect for the massive columns and the stern librarians of the Geelong City Library prevailed, and I sneaked it back on to the hall table, imperilling her innocence.

Reading the books she read only increased the mystery—all those fragments of conversation, all those names, all those snippets of information washing around in her head, and no way of knowing what she made of any of it. So I moved from texts to artefacts, as I'd say now. On the pretext of 'tidying her room'—a self-consciously girlish performance designed to gain access to otherwise inaccessible territory—I would handle the things she handled every day: comb, brush with her wavy dark hairs and stiffer silver ones tangled in it, and her three aids to beauty, the pot of Pond's Vanishing Cream, the face powder with its grimy puff, the dark red lipstick. I would pick them up, examine them, reflect on them. Metaphoric lips compressed, they would stare dumbly back.

This whole spying business only came back to me recently when I recognised the remains of another artefact of hers—or, more precisely, an artefact of Her—in the back room of the Anglesea beach house. I have no recollection of how it got to be there or into its present sorry condition, but now it is a dwarfish structure of a pile of three drawers topped by paired small ones, and above them a shelf closed by leadlight doors, once intended for hats.

Now the top and sides have lost their thick walnut veneer and are raw wood, with a piece of batik tossed over them. Once they were the core of the wardrobe which filled an entire wall of her bedroom. (Which points to another insoluble mystery: what happens to the furniture of childhood, so much more substantial than any furniture encountered afterwards? It is solid as elephants, yet it evaporates in a moment.)

Having failed to penetrate the living subject, the wardrobe became my icon and image of my mother—a fixed and examinable model of the elusive Other, a palace of secrets. On the very few occasions when my mother went out and left me alone I would fly to it. The heavy paired drawers which took up the full width of the bottom—vanished now, who knows where?—could be understood as her feet. I think one drawer actually did have an accumulation of old shoes in it. But feet, even her feet, did not interest me. I knew them well, anyway, because I used to give her pedicures.

Interest began with the three central drawers. The lowest held her corsets, savage constructions for all their flesh-pink satin, with their stabbing bones and toothed metal hooks, and yet much more my mother's body than the pallid flesh they gathered in to make her own proper shape. They retained her basic body smell: sweat, Lux soap, an undertang of rubber. They held no deeper mystery for me because I often helped her into them, pulling hard on the long strings and watching her creation by corset: the flat parabola of the behind without the least hint of cleavage, the drum-hard cross-laced front, the slight indent of the waist shaped by straining, shining fabric. With the last lace tied she would expel a long breath and stand for a moment, fully fashioned, impregnable, and I would feel the pride and the faint dismay of any squire watching his slouching daily companion transform into a knight.

The brassieres were altogether less formidable: softer, looser and comprehensively depressing. Surely my smooth boniness could never come to that? The next drawer was underwear, bloomers and singlets in white or pink cotton or yellowish wool, spartan stuff, admitting nothing. The one above held working skirts and cardigans—thready blues and duns, familiar as dirt—and her good navy blue with the anchor buttons.

At the top, equally taciturn but redolent with mystery because so rarely seen, were her hats: either the black straw or the brown felt, the absent one having gone out on her head, and the fawn leghorn with the dark velvet ribbon for best. I felt proud of my mother when she wore that hat. Above the wardrobe, piled nearly to the ceiling, was a stack of old travelling cases, whose smooth coats of silky dust confirmed my opinion that forever and forever there was and would be only Here. Behind the long thin doors flanking the drawers, on the left side, limp as dejected fairies, her four dresses, two wool jersey, two in some parodic version of silk and, on the right, military on their padded hangers, her winter coat and her good grey costume.

It was the small twinned drawers below the hats that I would leave until last and approach with a dry mouth, because they represented, according to the architectural body-map of the wardrobe, my mother's heart, her secret being.

The one on the right held a clutter of old photographs, some of them ink-stained, some foxed, and nearly all of them of people I did not recognise. For breathless months I was sure that the photographs held the coded message which would betray her real history and so her real nature. They say that children fantasise that they are foundlings, imposed like baby cuckoos on dull domestic folk by glamorous exotics—gipsies or circus people or royal fugitives or some alien tribe—who are prevented by a malicious fate from retrieving their lustrous offspring. I never thought that. However unimaginable the actual moment and process, I accepted that I was the fruit of my parents' loins. It was my mother's origins I had my doubts about. So I subjected those enigmatic photographic representations to hours of secret study, estimating possible degrees of intimacy, conjuring probable relationships—the dark lean man in the deckchair husband to the woman with the racquet, the girl in the cloche pulled down to her eyebrows sister to the boy waving to the camera, and nurturing an unspoken tenderness for the tall youth with the lank blond hair propped negligently to her left.

My mother? She was somewhere just off camera, or perhaps at the end of the long pale shoes and crossed ankles on the chaise-longue. Or was she the person they were all looking at, waving to, posing for? Was she the presence behind the camera? That's where I decided she was—not visible, but central. It did not worry me that the only camera in the house was my sister's Box Brownie, that my mother had never betrayed the least interest in or understanding of the photographic art. She wouldn't, would she?

One August afternoon, when my mother was bed-bound with the remains of flu, I slyly suggested that we might look at the photographs in the right-hand drawer, so I could put them in order, perhaps even label them. She agreed, amiably. So I dealt her worn pasteboard secrets out on the cream chenille one by one, watching her face like a fortune-teller, although it was not her future but her past I was after.

She watched, benignly, picked out a few, laughed at a hat—the girl in the cloche—shuffled a casual handful, and let them drop. 'You know, I can't remember a single one of these people. They're from holidays from years ago, before I was married, before I met Tom. Whatever possessed me to keep them so long? Might as well throw them out, they're just rubbish. Do you think you could manage to make a cup of tea?' I was not yet routinely trusted with boiling water.

I made the tea, but didn't throw out the photographs. I gathered them up, put them back in the drawer. I didn't believe her story for a moment. She had eluded me again. But I thought she had hesitated, just for a moment, at a badly foxed studio portrait of a young man, in profile, handsome, with a high forehead and dark waving hair brushed straight back. That one at least was no holiday snapshot.

It was the other drawer, the left side, the heart side, that promised most, because it held the things my mother herself had designated valuable by the act of putting them in there: a silver-mesh purse of her mother's, two white lace-edged handkerchiefs, a jet necklace, a string of greyish pearls, and three paisley chiffon scarves. It was the scarves that mattered most, for two reasons: they were cheap, unlike the other things, and they contained a faint, exotic smell. Her face-powder, a trace of her sweat—those were familiar. But, behind that, something else. Roses? Cinnamon? A hot smell which somehow seemed to be inherent in the texture of the fabric itself, in its harshness against mouth and nostrils. Was it India hiding there?

I do not have the scarves—they have evaporated, in the way treasured trivial things do. But I know my childhood is hidden in them. Even now, if I breathe deep, deep, I can smell my mother's scarves, a frail olfactory ghost dancing on the rim of consciousness. I still cannot identify its nature or its country of origin.

I was mostly content to spy, and sometimes to question. I made only one experiment, and that a failed one. I used my first wages, earned at eleven for being a runner in my father's factory, to buy the most luxurious gift I could find. It was a box of writing paper, deeply tinted, heavily scented, the whole facsimilating a plump pink heart-shaped cushion. End-of-war Geelong did not run to much in the way of exotica. It was mainly a love-gift, but I also hoped that the pure glory of the thing might break a lifetime's discretion; that at last my mother would write to some hitherto unrevealed and remarkable Someone.

The stratagem failed. She thanked me, admired it with just the right degree of awe—and put it away not in either one of the twin high-value drawers, but in the drawer for utilitarian underwear. I found it there the day after her funeral, pink and smug in its cellophane. She had outwitted me again.

Soon after the writing-box affair I lost interest in the whole campaign, as my marvellous mysterious mother shrank to the usual dwarfish grotesque concocted out of adolescent female censoriousness. But now I can see that my pursuit of her has been a lifetime activity; that my early fascination with her impenetrability, and my pleasure in that impenetrability, has a great deal to do with my long happy life as a historian spent in pursuit of other more distant, less impervious impenetrabilities.

Thinking about the shape of her life also made me realise that I have lived through a revolution—a revolution so comprehensive as to be almost invisible. Although for a time we shared the narrow space of a shared roof, she lived in a different world. I take for granted my emancipation from serious physical labour, as from serious physical or emotional discomfort, which is why falling ill came as a surprise. It would not have surprised my mother. She always expected the worst.

I also assume my physical mobility, my social mobility, my intellectual mobility. I will speak in public without much worrying about it. My mother lived and died a quiet woman domestically and an invisible one publicly. She assumed only her right to adequate food, to rather less than adequate warmth—a kitchen stove in a weather-board house with floors covered in chilly linoleum. Otherwise she accepted a servant's place in a social world which was, from her perspective, as rigid as a Turk's—except for those few hours of freedom in the afternoon her literacy had won her. I am angry that her life was so constricted when mine has been so free.

Now, when I am not many years younger than she was when she died, I am still sifting my handfuls of sand, still trying to make them stand and hold a shape I could call 'my mother'. And still, for all my gatherings and pattings, she continues to fall apart like a sand lady. If she is on the beach at all she is a mirage, an eye-baffling dazzle fleeing before me, receding faster than I can run.

MIRAGES

In the course of my childhood-retrieving exercise I was troubled, first, by the unreality of the person invoked as 'me', and then by my implicit claim I still was that person merely grown larger. Am I that person? Is my consciousness really continuous? To put it more elaborately: it may not only be a question of whether I state my memories truthfully (sometimes), or whether I remember accurately (I do and I don't), but whether the 'I' is sufficiently continuous to claim possession of those early memories at all.

The self, the sense of self and the way memory works all change through time. Psychologists say that after the age of about seven, children remember in narratives, just as adults do, but before that they remember in snapshots, vivid visual moments with little to connect them. That seems true for me. I know that when I wrote my first memory-story about Herbie and the baker I found I needed to write it in the third person, to reflect the conscious process of retrieval I had to go through to piece the vivid fragments together.

Then come the invisible transformations wrought by accumulating experience, and the development of a conscious narrative of the self—which again will change through time. Christopher Isherwood raised the point years ago, reflecting on the relationship between the older, bleaker Christopher and the naive young man setting out on his first journey abroad thirty years before:

> And now before I slip back into the convention of calling this young man 'I', let me consider him as a separate being, a stranger almost...For, of course, he is almost a stranger to me. I have revised his opinions, changed his accent and his mannerisms, unlearnt or exaggerated his prejudices and his habits. We still share the same skeleton, but its outer covering has altered so much that I doubt if he would recognise me on the street. We have in common the label of our name, and a continuity of consciousness; there has been no break in sequence of daily statements that I am I. But what I am has refashioned itself throughout the days and years, until now almost all that remains constant is the mere awareness of being conscious...
>
> The Christopher who sat in that taxi is, practically speaking, dead; he only remains reflected in the fading memories of us who knew him...I can only reconstruct him from his remembered acts and words and from the writings he has left us...In a sense he is my father, and in another sense my son...

This is at once completely persuasive, and rather too disquieting to live with. (It is also, you will agree, marvellously well put.) As I tap it out, I realise that it was this passage, read years ago, not then comprehended but never forgotten, which has led me into my present fix of trying to reconstruct something of the thoughts and anxieties of the smaller creature with whom I share a name, a vague continuity of awareness, some memories—and possibly very little else.

Reconstructed childhoods easily become works of dramatic art. Elie Wiesel, engulfed by the Holocaust in adolescence, remembers his childhood as 'a sunny and mysterious place where beggars were princes in disguise, and fools were wise men freed from their constraints'. The tragic surprise that history had in store for him, the terrible parabola of his life thereafter, the plunge into the abyss, required that his life-narrative have a magically happy beginning, an infinity of promise.

My moderately sunny and quite unthreatened childhood held no beggars, no fools, no wise men and no princes either, in disguise or out of it. On the contrary: everyone, child or adult, appeared to me remarkably fluid, inhabiting their various social roles with dismaying lightness of being.

The two great twentieth-century hunt-masters of memory, Marcel Proust and Vladimir Nabokov, have very different notions regarding the nature of their quarry and how to catch it. For Nabokov memory is an act of will. He believes he holds the delectable images and sensations of his childhood—the slur of snow under a sleigh, the exact shades of Russia's taffeta winter skies, the sound of his mother's silken skirts, the citrus fragrance of her skin—stored in the inviolable crystal of his mind, where they will be safe forever, provided he does not let the dust of the vulgar seep in. But we have to wonder: was it the total eclipse of the imperial Russian past which sets the people of his childhood glowing like icons in amber? Madame Nabokov fades once the Revolution whisks away her glorious setting. Neither we nor her son quite recognise the scented creature of his youth in the quiet old lady living among her relics in a dusty Paris room.

Proust is an ardent materialist. For him the past is stored in some material object, to be miraculously liberated (the liberation usually being attended by an effusion of joy) through an involuntary association generated by a providential sensation—the taste of a madeleine dunked in herb tea, the scent of a cheap chiffon scarf. Scents deny the passage of time, the extinction of the past. The photographs Claude Levi-Strauss took on his Brazilian expedition had little to say to him fifty years later, but he had only to open his old notebooks and release the ghost of the creosote he used to protect his canteens from termites, and presto! the miracle: 'Almost undetectable after more than half a century, this trace instantly brings back to me the savannas and forests of Central Brazil, inseparably bound with other smells—human, animal, and vegetable— as well as with sounds and colours.'

However firmly rejected by experts and artists, the folk notion of the sludge of daily memory resting quietly until stirred into life by some accidental stimulus is often vindicated by experience. The surge of blood into my father's brain in the last year of his life tossed him back into the churned battlefields of France, as if the explosion in his head had effected an equivalent explosion in memory so that what had been decently buried for decades was brought writhing, horribly, to the surface. After the transplant my own mind, agitated by the leaking of chemicals into the brain, tossed up living fragments of my own deep memory which I did not even recognise as mine, until they began their parade behind my eyelids.

The stimulus need not be dramatic. Proust was right about that. The insidious intrusion might come with no more than a nudge— the ghost of a tune, the trace of a scent. One ordinary evening a friend dining with us excused himself to go to the bathroom. He returned dazed and slightly panicky: for no good reason, washing his hands in a Kew bathroom, the cup of the Now had fractured and he had been catapulted back into the China he had left a decade before. A shaking experience, quite enough to trick a man into superstitious reverence for unappeased spirits. Yet not remarkable after all. We found the culprit sitting in the soap dish—a tablet of Flower and Bee sandalwood soap, imported from China, and holding within it his own younger, more hopeful self. So perhaps we are layers, after all. Perhaps nothing is ever lost.

For me, as I think for most of us who do not solicit memory for aesthetic or voluptuous or dramatic ends but who yearn after the trout-gleam of truth, memory is less a crystal than an eel, wily, evasive, as hard to hold as any truly vital thing. It might come stealthily, a slow, irresistible leak from the crammed past snaking its way into the featureless present, but once liberated it is irrepressible. But while I have always known it to be slippery (historians make a living from mistrusting it), it was only when the unnatural solitude of illness made memory my full-time companion that I came to appreciate the depths of its character defects—its unreliability, its affront at being questioned, its rage at being impugned, its incorrigible complacency even when caught out.

I have a vivid recollection of my Aunt Rose confiding to me that she visited my defunct Uncle Paul in Kew cemetery every day, to talk with him. I can hear her sincere, raggy little voice, see her proud, embarrassed eyelids, feel my own embarrassment—why is she telling me this?—as she tells me. I know where she told me: in the afternoon dimness of her bedroom, with the white quilt on the dark bed, the yellow roses and their fallen petals on the dressing-table shining in a last shaft of sun. But that moment could not have happened, because nowadays I roam the Kew cemetery, and I found a gravestone there which tells me that Aunt Rose died seven years before her husband.

It is hard to argue with graven stone. I think now that I must have dreamt that afternoon conversation. I am often confused by the plausible realism of my dreams, meeting someone in the morning I had mourned and buried the previous night. But I cannot erase it merely because I know it to be untrue. It is still part of my experience, of aunts, of houses, of a certain kind of marriage: part of my unreliable, essential, personal record, and so part of my unreliable, essential, personal self.

Unreliable selves. While I wrote the essays on my parents as honestly as I was able, I knew my account to be miserably inadequate. We build up our pictures of people intimately known by a kind of pointillism, a thousand flecks of experience laid on the canvas, without much intervention from the conscious mind. When we think of them, that is what is evoked: a roughly bounded sea of possibilities emerging out of points of light. Anything we actually say about them must seem a grotesque simplification, a spiteful denial of a unique ambience, and the infinite freedoms conferred by exigency. Only fiction can redress the existential ambiguities which stalk the real world.

REPRISE

Now I am close to normal health, I go on writing, still with a sense of urgency. Now I know how little time there is.

After years of doing it I think I am beginning to understand the work of writing history—the how of it, the why of it—but I still don't understand the work of writing fiction. There is a Spanish saying of which I am unreasonably fond: 'No hay reglas,' 'There are no rules here.' That is the way fiction seems to me. If there are rules, I don't know them.

Engagement with professional history imposes rules. One of those rules is that we must represent our chosen people as justly and completely as we are able. We must try to understand them, and for that we need a supple imagination, but that is imagination's only role. With history I am bound like Gulliver by a thousand gossamers: epistemologically to the deceitful, accidental record, morally to the dead men and women I have chosen to re-present, and to the living men and women I want to read my words and to trust them.

In history there is no necessary shape to a story. We begin and end our telling where we choose. Where does the story of Mr Robinson begin? Where would we find the origins of his stubbornness, his energy, his susceptibility to the attraction of the unfamiliar? Where would we search out the impulses which brought him and his free compatriots to so alien a land? Where would this story end? He speaks to us and moves us still. Like life, history is always shadowed by mystery.

With fiction it is different. I see an old lady walking briskly along a beach, a lumpish boy huddling against the rain in a park, the quivering reflection of a girl's face in a train window, and these are gifts to be played with as I choose. The shape of a story blooms in my head, I cherish it for a while, imagine my way through it, set it down. Fiction invents a world free from moral demands and from moral consequences, while imposing paradoxical restrictions of its own. We may invent experiences and put our chosen shapes upon them, but the experiences must always be believable, which is something history does not require. Who could have invented the Black Hole of Calcutta, the siege at Krishnapur? Who could have imagined Hitler and the twelve-year rule of the Thousand Year Reich? Fiction pretends that humans are simpler, more stable, more predictable than they are.

Fiction also affords the pleasure of the effortless penetration of fellow humans who are in the real world chronically enigmatic. We know our own feelings towards intimates. In time we learn their proclivities. But we also know their ultimate opacity—or discover it catastrophically. With fiction I turn into vapour, float through bone, look out through other eyes.

The hallucination narratives form a category of their own. I played no concious role in their making: I simply transcribed them, turning their unbearably vivid sequences of images into words which seemed implicit, indeed immanent, in the actions. There was no sense of choice as to words or sequence—just the feverish impulse to record.

As for memory—memory is the vast steppe between history and fiction. It is by nature Janus-faced: it looks back to the expansiveness and the mystery of history, forward to the elegance of invention. It is at once as flexible as a contortionist and as intransigent as a Hussar: it insists both on its right to participate in history's authority—'Thus It Was'—and in the glitter and vamp of fiction.

History might begin with experience, but if it is to become authentic history, treasured memories must be rigorously, ruthlessly analysed and evaluated.

Fiction might begin from experience, from random moments or the complicated knot of past experiences out of which our present selves are constituted, but if it is to be true fiction the experience must be utterly transformed in the telling, and made into a thing suffused by the distinctive kind of pleasure—a complex mix of completeness, precision of statement and surprise—we call aesthetic delight.

LILLIT AND OTHER STORIES

BETWEEN STATIONS

Begin with a train, creeping sleek as a millipede across the flat land which lies to the north-west of the city of M.

In the third compartment there sits a girl. A small, moist-looking creature, she is pretty in a damp kind of way. She is also unhappy: her knees are pressed together and her ankles pushed apart so that her toes can cuddle through the leather. It is just possible to see the meek curve of her right breast under the thin cloth of her grey coat.

The sliding door crashes open. A man enters; a large man, looking larger because he is wearing a wide-brimmed, earth-coloured hat. He tosses the hat up on to the rack, and sits down.

So now the man and the girl are sitting on the same leatherette seat. Train seats are fine communicators, picking up the sigh of a shifted buttock, the taffeta squeak of a sideways shuffle.

This time not a buttock flexes. Instead the night sweeps down and curtains the windows and the grimy compartment waves its electric wand and becomes a cosy room for two rocking through black flowing space.

The girl relaxes by staring into the blackness of the window-become-mirror. She is watching her ghostly face wobbling and wavering between the yellow-lit compartment and the rushing night, and as she stares into the ghostly eyes they begin to grow a rippling silvery rim, like the underside of a fish, and each fish gathers and swells and makes its tiny trout-leap over the rim of the lid, slides over the plump of cheek, and with a joyful wriggle and slither nests in the depression at the corner of her mouth where her mournful tongue gathers it up.

She is now unequivocally damp. The man, guessing at the tears from the faint tremble of the leatherette, is frightened by the weeping but moved by the decorous knees and the childish toes, and the gentle, infinitely dolorous curve of the right breast (the only one he can see) under the thin fabric of the grey coat.

So he slides along the swooning leatherette, and says, 'Excuse me, but are you all right?'

He is holding in his large blunt hand a bouquet of Kleenex. He is looking into the girl's right ear, turned to him like an oriental flower.

It is pretty enough as ears go—rim curled, interior walls sleek, the vortice itself appropriately whorled, the heart an ivory mystery. I admit the lobe is charming: tiny, plump, it is its own tender pearl.

It is, nonetheless, only an ear. But in the same instant the man has seen the thin hand lying open, abandoned on the bench, and there flashes on his inner vision the image of a small, wounded animal, and he feels a sudden painful constriction in his throat, and looks again at the ear. And is lost.

The girl turns her head. The face is unremarkable: round, eyelashes stuck into wet star-shapes, eyes and nostrils pink-edged, pouting lips beginning to smile. What luck! But the damage is done, the arrow has flown, he is transfixed. He understands several things he has never understood before. He understands that this girl, this marvellous creature wrapped in grey fabric and damp skin, feels the blood in her fingertips, breathes, dreams, trembles. That she is alive, exactly as he is alive. And that he need never be alone again. He had never thought himself alone before.

What happens next? What matters has already happened. How will it end? Badly. A large stolid man has fallen victim to the feverish incapacitation we call love, he has fallen in love with an ear. How can it not end badly? How badly? There will be rage and despair and shouting and tears and fleshly pearls wearing the diamonds of betrayal, and a scalpel wielded by weeping, shaking hands…

I will tell you one thing. They have scarcely met. They have not yet touched each other. But they will never be as happy as they are now, in the small lit space in the sleek black train millipeding its way towards the provincial town of B, in the middle of the tired flat lands of the great north-western plain.

YALTA

1 April, My First Day. Yalta! It is more beautiful than I thought possible.

I have read 'the sea is blue', or 'the sea is green'. It is neither and both and more all at once—green and blue, grey and silver, gold and lilac, even pink. There is every colour in it, and every colour is changing. I will never tire of looking at it. Twenty years in this world, and my first sight of the sea! The town is wonderfully pretty, the buildings light and pale with the cupolas floating above them, and above the cupolas the mountains, which are bare and brown and ought to be ugly, but instead they shimmer, too. And every house and hotel has its garden and every street its palm trees and towards the sea there are cypresses, dark, dark green, almost blue, and their shadows on the white walls are violet. And flowers everywhere. There are camellia trees all around the public square, red and white, and every one of them in bloom and every bloom perfect. In April! R is still deep in mud and soot, and its gloomy skies leak rain every single day. Winter never seems to end there. Here I think it is always spring.

Now I am glad that Sergei sent me here instead of to St Petersburg. Of course I long to see Mama and Papa and Grigori (S says, 'All you ever say is "St Petersburg! St Petersburg! When I get to St Petersburg!"'). But not yet. Not until I am calmer. Already I feel more tranquil, and I am not the least lonely. Sergei warned me that the hotel 'was not of the first class' but it is much prettier than the grander ones, with arches and walkways and terraces and an inside courtyard where one may take one's morning coffee! My room has its own balcony with its own pot of bright red geraniums, and I need not have worried about the hotel people—they are lovely. When I arrived there were mandarins and white carnations on the writing table, and the *femme de chambre* (Sergei said I must practise my French 'in Yalta') waiting by the door, and positively beaming. Varenka is a little round creature no more than sixteen, and she giggles all the time. She giggled when she brought the basins and towels I needed to bathe Mouse, giggled through all the washing and drying and wriggling, giggled while she whisked everything away and mopped up the water (the floor is beautiful green tiles). I'm sorry to say I giggled too, but she was so funny, and so was Mouse. Varenka says she is in love with Mouse.

Also I think that at least one of Varenka's parents must be Tatar! Of course she is a Christian—she loves my icon—and her Russian is good, and she wears the proper starched pinafore and pleated cap, but her skin is a rose-gold colour, and her hair jet black, coarse, and very long: she plaits it and twists it and wears it like a black club between her shoulders. Mine is like spiderwebs beside it, so at first she brushed far too hard.

Mouse had to be bathed because on our very first day she has already been wicked, and she has also found a friend. She was sick for the whole crossing, quivering and trembling as much from fear as from seasickness, so as soon as we disembarked I sent the baggage on to the hotel (a Tatar in a red fez and striped jacket came to claim it) and took her for a walk along the Esplanade, and the little wretch leaped straight from the boards and onto the beach! At first she hated the sand sliding under her feet—she would pick up one paw after the other, shaking them most disdainfully—but then she discovered she could DIG, and the sand flew, and then a little red dog rushed up and began to dig too. They dug shoulder to shoulder for a while, then they chased each other—Mouse tossing me wicked black glances over her little white shoulder, daring me to catch her—and then her friend rushed into the sea, and without thinking what she was doing Mouse rushed after her! She bit the water because it dared to wet her, coughed and spluttered, and then she was barking at the ripples and chasing seagulls as if she had been a water dog all her life. I think I will have to buy a lead. She was always so good on her walks in R, but there are so many distractions in Yalta.

Her new friend is very pretty and gay, with long silky ears and the sweetest expression, and her coat is glossy as a chestnut. Which is her name: I heard it when her master finally called her away. She ran directly to him—not like Mouse, who ignored me—and leapt straight into his arms, sandy and wet as she was, and he laughed and tousled her ears.

He is quite tall, slender, dark-haired, dark-eyed, quietly dressed. He carries a cane, and wears a dark cap. I am sure he is a gentleman.

So—Mouse had to be bathed on the balcony in a bowl of warm water and dried on one of the hotel's big white towels, while Varenka giggled.

Tomorrow I am to meet Madame Oleska. I am sure she is the reason why Sergei insisted I come here, why he made me spend so much money on clothes—and why he gave me this diary to keep: 'Anna, remember! Write down not only the names but the titles of the people you will meet at Madame Oleska's!' It is true I do not remember titles very well. He hopes I will go to evening parties and meet important people. I hope I will not. I am afraid at those parties because everyone is so old and severe, and I do not know what to say to them, and one must stay for at least two hours. In any case this is my private diary and he may not read it, and I will write what I choose, just as I did at school—not the nonsense I wrote then, but a chronicle of events here, and of my own thoughts and feelings. I have hung the beautiful icon my mother gave me above the writing table. It will help me to be honest, and just.

I confess I do not understand myself very well. For these last months I have been unhappy, quite without reason. Sometimes I feel I cannot breathe—that life is smothering me. R is dull but, as Sergei says, after St Petersburg any provincial town will seem dull. He also says we must expect provincial postings for many years yet.

He also says I will become accustomed to married life, now I have the house and the piano, and he has given me Mouse for company 'until the children come'. Children. I don't think I'm ready for children.

He is very patient with me.

The last thing he said as the bell rang and the train pulled out was, 'Remember, Madame Oleska's husband is a *Councillor*!' What kind of councillor I do not know. What I do know is that the note she sent round to the hotel tells me we are to meet on the Esplanade at 11 a.m. tomorrow. On the Esplanade! I suppose she wants to be sure I am not a Tatar before she invites me to her house.

I will wear the linen with the long jacket, the grey kid boots and my grey beret. And the lilac parasol.

Second Day. When we met Madame Oleska told me to 'turn around so I can look at you'. On the Esplanade, with everyone watching.

Madame Oleska is large, and decorates her largeness with a great many ruches and flounces. She speaks loudly and much of the time in French, which I cannot understand even though Mademoiselle always said my French was very good.

Sergei has met Madame Oleska only once, at a musical evening at the Panshin house in St Petersburg. Doubtless she would have dressed and conducted herself more quietly there. He remembered her as 'very gracious'. I do not think she is gracious. She is *exactly like Fraülein Grüner*—even to the ruches!

We walked for the best part of an hour in the gardens and the square, but even though she was constantly nodding and bowing scarcely anyone nodded back, and not one person stopped to speak to us. I was very much embarrassed.

She also has a very disagreeable dog. Madame O says Chou-Chou is a Pomeranian, but she does not look the least like Mouse, being twice as big and very ugly, with tufty orange hair and weepy red eyes, and she snaps at everyone, including Madame O. Mouse was terrified of her. She spent the whole morning trembling in my arms or pressed against my boots.

As for tomorrow, Madame O informs me that she 'does not want me in the morning' but I am to be waiting at the hotel entrance at two o'clock. She will call for me in her carriage. We are to go for a drive.

This afternoon I dined in my room and watched the sun set behind the mountains. The food is wonderful here—and it is not necessary to fight the cook first! Even the kasha is delicious. And the waiter (Fyodor) brought me a little bottle of wine without my asking. He told me there is a famous waterfall close to Yalta, and that Madame O will probably take me there.

In Yalta the sky is dark indigo when the stars begin to come out. How they blaze!

A week ago I thought I was dying. My heart fluttered; I could not draw my breath. Now, after only two days here, I am well again. I do not feel I am choking, I even laugh. What does it mean? Why was I so ill in R? Sergei says I 'needed a change of air', that the effluvia and fogs do not suit my lungs. It is true that even now I can taste the wet soot. But I do not think it is the air. It feels like guilt, or grief. Yet I have done nothing wrong, and no-one is dying.

Mouse was asleep in her basket before she finished her milk. Her legs are twitching. She is dreaming of seagulls. Varenka brought her an extra cushion, a red and yellow striped satin one, and a yellow blanket. It is like having a little Tatar baby in the room.

It is very late, but lanterns are still moving in the street below.

Third Day. I am exhausted and frantic and angry and ashamed. A terrible, terrible day.

It began beautifully: Mouse and I went down to watch the morning steamer come in. It is a local entertainment here—last night Fyodor told me that half Yalta goes down to see who is disembarking, who they are with, what they are wearing. When I asked him if he ever goes down he laughed and said never.

It was indeed delightful, with the air clear and the bay shining and the fishing boats bobbing, and then the steamer with its flags and the people pouring off, waving to their friends, laughing and embracing among the luggage (Tatars scrambling everywhere), and then sorting themselves into carriages and whirling away. I saw at least three ladies of fashion. I do not think I can wear my grey voile here. The waist is too high.

I felt a little lonely after all the welcoming, and then, when everyone was gone, there were Chestnut and her master only two benches away! The dogs leapt into their little ritual at once: run in circles for one minute, dance for two, dig for three, then pelt off to terrify the seagulls.

Meanwhile Chestnut's master and I sat on our respective benches and gazed at the sea.

I do not think he was waiting for anyone any more than I was. I think he likes the hubbub and then the quietness, and then looking at the sea. He looks tranquil, and kindly, but there is an air of melancholy about him. And he is pale. Perhaps he has been ill. Yalta is full of invalids, Fyodor said, rolling his eyes. The air was already warm, but the gentleman kept his coat buttoned to the chin, and he leant his head against the back of the seat as if he were weary.

Of course I did not look directly at him. I was able to observe him through the fringe of my parasol (the cream one). Then he called Chestnut, smiled at Mouse, touched his cap to me, and slowly walked away.

Mouse and I looked at the sea for a time, and then went back to the hotel. She is not brave enough to chase the seagulls on her own.

Madame O arrived at half-past two in a closed carriage pulled by a great raw-boned beast which champed and tossed its head about and which her coachman seemed quite unable to control. It transpires that Madame O is thinking of buying the horse, wanted to try it out, and thought she would give me a treat at the same time! At least she left Chou-Chou at home. She thought the ride would be 'too rough' for her.

We lurched out of the town, all of it pretty as far as I could see from the jolting cell we were in, with charming buildings and flowers everywhere—and then in a flash the buildings and the prettiness were gone and we were in a sad flat land of scraped-looking earth, fine white dust, thin little horses and general misery. We came to a village and dashed into it, much too fast—the children barely had time to spring away from our wheels—and then the horse was dragged to a stop so I could examine the people—*'les barbares turcs'*, as Madame O called them!

It was a Tatar village, the huts strangely shaped and very poor, with not a blade of grass anywhere, and everything filmed with that strange white dust which lifts with the least wind and sifts everywhere—back at the hotel I found my boots were white with it. I saw no women and only four men, but those four frightened me. They stared at us, as if we were trees or stones, not humans at all. One was wearing a long open coat of the same red and yellow satin as Mouse's cushion. Perhaps they worked on the wharves or even in the hotels, but I think those men hated us.

I was very glad that Madame O decided not to step down. Yet the children looked merry enough, their brown faces grinning at us out of their cocoons of rags.

The village is called Autka. Just beyond it the land rises a little and suddenly there is a dense forest, a real one of the kind that would be full of mushrooms in autumn, and then, just as suddenly, a green oasis where a gentleman's house is being built. Madame O ordered the coachman to stop, which he did with his usual horrible jerk so that foam flew from the poor brute's mouth. Presumably the house was what we had come to see.

It is a strange house, or an unusual one, painted white and full of odd angles, and it clings to the side of the mountain as if it is about to come tumbling down. I could see why it had been built like that, with lots of windows, and balconies jutting everywhere—for the views. Some would let you look out to the forest, some to the mountains, and others to Yalta and the bay. It would be wonderful to live there and watch the mountains and the sea through all the changes of the day.

The garden is not long laid out but it is charming, with young tulips peeking out from their hay and the bright green spikes of baby palms set out along the walks. From the road we could see a little stream with a lopsided wooden bridge crossing it, an old willow turned young by the spring, and an orchard crammed with new orange and lemon trees, mulberry and quince, and what looked like rows of peach and apricot trees already buried in drifts of white blossom. But the wonder of the place is a huge, huge tree at the very front of the house, every twig of it smothered with crisp dark red flowers with long yellow stamens, and the bees all wild with joy—we could hear them roaring, and even from the carriage I could smell the honey. It made me breathless to look at it, it was so beautiful.

Madame O said it was an almond tree. Would an almond tree grow so very large? And surely almond blossoms are white?

Madame O is always full of information, but I suspect her information is not always correct.

And then we heard a long, wailing cry which made me jump, and it was the muezzin from Autka calling his fellow villagers to prayer! I thought it beautiful, the high, wild cry caught and flung back by the mountains, but Madame O said it was a disgrace, that our Tsar should not permit the worship of false gods on Russian soil. I do not see why the Tatars should be deprived of their mosques and their religion—they lived here first, and they are poor enough already. And surely it must be our same God, with a different name. But of course I did not say any of this, for Sergei's sake.

Then Madame O looked for her watch buried somewhere among the ruches, and shrieked at the coachman to turn and to get back to town because she was expecting people to dine at four o'clock and it was by now well past that. He lashed at the horse, the carriage lurched around, we were flung everywhere, there was a great jerk—and suddenly a most piteous yelping. The horse had stepped on a dog! It had come running out from the new garden, a blur of red, and I was sure it was Chestnut! I begged Madame O to stop so I could get down to tend her, and she positively screamed at me, 'Stay where you are!' and '*Vite, Vite!*' at the coachman, and we were scattering the children in the village and lurching through the dust towards Yalta.

I was very angry and shocked that we should have left a creature we ourselves had injured helpless on the road, although for Sergei's sake I tried not to show it.

Madame O filled the time as we rushed back by telling me about the man who lives in the house at Upper Autka, or sometimes lives there: she says he is often away. The ridiculous stories came spilling out. He is a doctor. No, he is a writer; he writes vulgar stories for the Moscow press. He is a doctor and a writer but his grandfather was a serf and his father a bankrupt. He is a nihilist; he spent years at a penal colony in Siberia. He writes stories, but he also writes plays and hires actors to act them and makes money from them. What kind of plays? The kind no sensible person would want to see. Why not? Because they are full of people who never do anything sensible, who never do anything at all. Nothing happens in them, there's no jokes, no songs, and no philosophy either, just a lot of talk and people putting on and taking off their gloves, and then suddenly shooting each other. Has she seen any of these plays? No: she would not dream of going, and anyway they are staged in Moscow in the winter when she is here. And furthermore this doctor-writer had not even answered her invitation—'Handwritten! In French!'—to attend one of her musical evenings, so of course he is not worth knowing. As for the house: he built it for his mother, he fills it with actresses, gipsies and other disreputables, most of them 'not even from Yalta'. And he has had a telephone installed. This seemed to irritate her exceedingly. She has no telephone herself: she 'does not feel the need of it'.

She left me at the hotel entrance at half-past four—ordering me to jump down and not to wait for the steps, as if I were sixteen and not a married woman—and drove away complaining loudly to the street in general that I had made her late for her friends.

I will not see her again. Sergei will be angry but I will not. She treats me like a child, a stupid, backward child, and I cannot, will not bear it. I do not care how important she and her councillor are, she is a rude and ignorant person—taking me out in such a cart behind such a horse to stare at those poor villagers, then at the private house of a gentleman she does not know and about whom she speaks such nonsense. And then injuring Chestnut! But even had that half-wild animal not stepped on Chestnut I could not bear her.

Should she wish to see me again I shall certainly have a headache.

I hope she does not write to Sergei.

Of course she will not. I have done nothing wrong.

I am ill again. I feel as if I cannot breathe, as if there is a weight on my breast so that my heart must beat in my throat. It beats so fast!

I would pray for Chestnut but I do not know if it is permitted to pray for a dog. I will pray for her master instead. Tomorrow I must try to find him, to explain and to beg his forgiveness.

Mouse is snoring already. I doubt I shall sleep tonight.

Fourth Day. Mouse and I were awake very early, and after breakfast we went straight down to the waterfront. I hoped we would meet Chestnut's master, and that I would have the courage to speak to him, to inquire about Chestnut, and to ask his pardon. The morning was calm, with the sea no-colour like new pewter and a mist rising from it and the water clear. I could see the shadows of little fish in the shallows. Mouse chased them for a while. But we were restless, Mouse and I, and he did not come.

Then, with the steamer in sight, he came running down the quay. His coat was unbuttoned, he looked pale, and so wild I dared not approach him. He was carrying a loose bouquet of yellow tulips.

The steamer berthed, the gangplank was lowered. And she arrived.

She is of medium height, rather swarthy and not at all pretty. She has a deep, deep voice which carries well, makes large gestures, and she is always moving and talking. She is obviously an actress.

There was another woman with her whom he ignored at first, then he embraced her—and then he turned back to the first one. He smiled as she let a tulip fall, and smiled more as she bent to pick it up and dropped four others.

When he looks at her his heart is in his eyes.

I think she is too active and too noisy for a sick man.

I saw Madame O on the Esplanade this afternoon. She nodded, very coolly, and passed on, and so did I. I am glad to be rid of her.

I cannot always be hiding in the hotel or at the sea. Tomorrow I will explore the shops and dine at the restaurant in the square.

Sergei said that 'while I was in Yalta with nothing to do' I should read some novels 'to improve my conversation', and so I shall. Fyodor says there is an excellent bookshop here. We were not permitted to read novels at school, and in R there seems to be no time for reading. Fyodor suggests I should read *Anna Karenina* by our great Russian writer Count Tolstoy. He says I will enjoy it. I hope so. I have heard that Count Tolstoy is a solemn old gentle-man, and I am sad enough already.

There was a great blue butterfly lying on the terrace this evening. I think it was dying. I wanted to carry it inside so the birds would not peck it, but it was furry and quivering, and I could not bring myself to touch it. I am a shameful coward.

Fifth Day. This morning I went into Vernet's for an ice—lovely long silver spoons that go all the way to the bottom of the glass—and then found the bookshop and the book, and I read a little of it on the balcony, and indeed I do like it. The descriptions are lovely.

At dinner today (in the square at last, how brave) Mouse did something she has never done before: for no reason at all she growled at the gentleman at the next table, who was waving his finger at her. And then she growled again! I was ashamed of her. I could feel my face getting hot as I explained that she did not bite. The gentleman laughed and said she had not frightened him too badly, and tried to give her a bone. Which she would not take.

We talked a little, and when he had taken away the plates the waiter brought the gentleman's coffee to my table. His name is Dmitri Dmitrich Gurov. He is from Moscow, quite old, a banker, on holiday here for a few weeks. His wife and children are in Moscow, because the children must go to school. His daughter is only five years younger than I am!

He is perhaps a little stout, but he is gentleman-like and pleasant to talk to. He does not know the gentleman with the red dog. We are to meet for lunch tomorrow. He said that he is anxious to see the waterfall too, and that he would be honoured to escort me. I told him just a little about Madame Oleska, and he laughed and laughed, and said 'the woman was notorious'.

His manners are excellent. Mouse does not like him. I could feel her grumbling in her chest the whole time we were talking. But surely there can be no harm in lunching together—not in so public a situation. Not here. Not in Yalta.

LACE

We file off the bus, toddle along the path, pay our drachmas to the woman at the door, toddle inside. The Museum of Traditional Embroidery is in an ordinary house—not ordinary now, of course, but ordinary once, a peasant house. The first room is small and dark. The electric light is on, but it is still dark: the ceiling is low, much less than two metres, and the windows narrow as gunslots. On either side of the fireplace there are two wooden chairs. They are tiny, the seats low and narrow, the backs straight. They look unpleasantly penitential, as if used to strap down unruly children, or midgets with posture problems. We shuffle in, stand around, stare at the chairs, the empty fireplace. What are we meant to do?

It seems the woman is also the guide. She dismounts from her stool and starts to shout in her mad English, 'The women sit *here*'—banging a chair, we flinch—'for the winter.' All the women? For the whole winter? How long is the winter? Silent confusion.

'They sew!' Another bang. 'They sew for their merrege.'

We see a young girl folded on the horrible little chair, chin on knees, sewing something white.

Mr Barnes, who is famously brave, asks, 'And later? After merrege?'

She glares at him. 'They sew!'

He swallows, persists. 'Why?'

'For the *Berry*!'

The Berry. Our faces are frozen in comic-book expressions of respectful wonder, but she knows we do not understand. She snorts; we hang our heads.

'The *Berry*, the *Foonrool*!'

Ah! the Foonrool, of course, we understand! There is a flurry of nods and congratulatory murmurs.

Mr Barnes pushes his luck. 'Four chairs. Where are all the men?'

She looks at him, sighs, and says, very clearly, 'The men are fishing. They are fishing'—she pauses, this is the *coup de grâce*—'they are fishing in the sea.'

She eyes him; he surrenders; she strides back to her stool. The guided bit of the tour is over.

Released, we drift into the other room. It is empty save for a long table. There are long white strips of embroidered cloth laid out on the table. The embroidery is also white. It is not possible to tell which pieces had to do with marriages and which with funerals; which shrouded brides, which veiled corpses. They are all equally ecclesiastical, all equally pristine.

The stitches are demonically small, the designs severe. They repeat themselves, over and over again.

The women sit sewing in the small dark room. The men are fishing in the sea.

FIRST MAN, FIRST WOMAN AND DOG

Hear how in the first days First Man lived in a cave with Dog as his only companion. Every night they would sleep in the cave, happy for the company, and every day they would go out to hunt. They would go out very early, when they were stiff with cold and full of hope, and as the day grew older they would grow warmer and less hopeful, but they nearly always brought meat back to the cave, and they always enjoyed themselves, and had many interesting experiences.

The nights were less enjoyable. Usually they would get back too late for First Man to think about finding dry wood and leaves and whirling firesticks to make a fire, and they would fetch up eating their meat raw. First Man might fumble around trying to smooth out the sour knot the sleeping skins had got themselves into, Dog might tug at a corner of the knot for a moment with her pretty white teeth and give it a playful little shake, but then they would just flop down close to each other to keep one side warm, and they'd be so tired after the hunting they'd fall asleep, but soon they would wake out of dreams of being hugged to death by giant ice-covered sloths or licked like ice-creams by ice-tongued leopards, and they would lie cold and shivering until the dawn and the time to go out into the dewy morning and begin the hunt.

Then one day, just after they had killed a pig, First Man noticed that Dog had vanished. First Man barked and yowled for a while, but Dog did not come back, so First Man picked up the pig and carried it back to the cave by himself. He didn't enjoy the walk home at all now he was tired, now that the hunting was over, and he missed Dog who made the long walk short by jumping on lizards, tossing them in the air, and swallowing them whole, grinning at him as the wriggling tail went down.

Just as he got back to the cave Dog came running out of the bush wagging her tail and dancing on all four furry feet. First Man shouted at her; what did she mean by running off like that? But then he forgot about being angry because he saw something remarkable. Inside the cave a fine fire was well alight, the earth floor had been brushed clear of bones, and his sleeping skins had been untangled and fluffed up to make a deep, soft pile, just waiting for his shaggy person.

So he and Dog threaded some pig meat on to a slim green sapling and scorched it until it was running with fat and juices, and ate it, and went to bed full and greasy, warm and happy.

The next day, just after Dog had run down a spotted hare and dropped it at First Man's feet, off she dashed again. First Man was angry, and wondered how he could persuade her to stand still long enough for him to give her a good beating. He trudged back to the cave on his wide brown feet, thinking grumbling thoughts to himself. But as he got to the clearing Dog appeared from the bushes. She was carrying some green herbs in her mouth, herbs which, he remembered, grew under the fourth hill down and which went remarkably well with hare. And again the cave was warm and bright with fire, the floor swept, the sleeping skins in a neat person-and-dog-shaped pile, while a great slab of the pig meat from the previous day was slowly roasting so that all the juices were sealed inside instead of making the small flames dance. Once again he and Dog ate well, and he quite forgot about wanting to beat her. Snuggled down among the skins with her furry back against his shaggy one, First Man knew that life was good.

But First Man was concerned with more than just eating and hunting and sleeping warm. He was curious, too. He wanted to understand, more or less, how the world worked. So he began to wonder who it could be who was cleaning the cave and lighting the fire and roasting the meat. Somebody was doing it. But there was only First Man and Dog in the entire place, so who could it be?

The next day they had a particularly thrilling time when First Man managed to spear a baby tapir in the lagoon while Dog snarled and slashed at the mother. (This is a Mapuche story; the Mapuche live in South America; tapirs live in South America.) After he had snatched up the baby tapir and run very fast for a very long time, mother tapirs being vengeful creatures, he was quite puffed out, and decided to cut straight back home to the cave. He'd quite lost track of Dog, but that often happened on a tapir hunt.

Back at the cave he saw a remarkable thing. He saw Dog come trotting out of the thickets with her feathery tail held high and her sleek red sides shining and her white teeth gleaming, and quick as a wink she had shrugged off her skin. A wriggle, and it was gone. And there in the clearing stood a beautiful smooth creature who in some ways looked like First Man, and in other ways didn't.

First Woman, for that is who it was, picked up the dog skin and spread it neatly on a bush close by the entrance of the cave and well out of the dust, and then she set to work. She worked very fast, *much* faster than you or I could do it, even faster than I can tell it, because she was, as you will have guessed by now, a creature in possession of serious magic. She scooped up a handful of leaves and twigs, whirled the fire-sticks between her smooth brown palms, and presto! a small bright flame was dancing between the stones. She took a big bundle of green leaves and brushed them over the floor, and where the leaves had passed the earth smelt sweet. She made a layer of those same aromatic leaves on top of some bracken, fluffed up the sleeping skins, and laid them on the leaves and bracken so they were sweet and springy. Then she reached right in under a deep cool bush and pulled out the hare Dog had caught the day before, now skinned and with the herbs tucked into its belly, skewered it, and propped it over the fire.

Then she looked around, nodded in a pleased way, whisked out of the cave, took a gourd full of water, poured it over herself to get rid of the dust, wriggled to get rid of the water, and was just about to slide back into the dogskin when First Man said, 'Hey! Wait! Hold on a minute! What's going on around here?'

So she told him. She told him that for as long as she was Dog she could go hunting with him and stay out all hours and chew raw meat with him and curl up at night with him and try to keep him warm, and dream about hunting. That was when she was Dog. When she was First Woman she could keep the cave tidy and cook the meat he caught and shake out the sleeping skins and keep all of him warm at night, and maybe in time when they got around to it she might give him a First Baby to play with.

But she couldn't do both. Either he could have a hunting companion, or he could have a Wife. First Man would have to choose. She would put on her dog skin and go and sit quietly at the cave entrance while he decided. And she did.

First Man thought, and he thought, and he *could not* decide. The next night he thought and he thought, and *still* he could not decide.

And that is why, even today, Dog prefers her meat cooked, although she will eat it raw if she is hungry, and why she is always eager to go off on a hunt; why she shakes herself, to see if her skin is still loose, and why she sometimes tosses the sleeping skins around, just for a moment, as if she is trying to remember something. And it is also why she sits at the entrance of the cave, and why she always keeps one eye on First Man, even when he is dozing beside his smoky little fire and his litter of old bones and stale sleeping skins, and why sometimes, just sometimes, she will slit her eyes and growl at him. Because the Mapuche say First Man is deciding still.

LILLIT

There is a child who comes to our house, a boy named Troy. He is perhaps five; he says he is five, then holds up four fingers. He comes because he is captivated by his reflection in the dark glass door. As he talks he watches his image and rehearses the ninja poses he picks up from television and from the older, tougher boy down the road, who takes karate lessons. In the glass they look like the dream-dances of a brain-damaged knight.

This kinetic conversation with his ideal self proceeds without reference to the conversation he is having with me, except that his talk is always heroically aspirational: 'Next year I will get an earring, a ninja outfit, a real motorbike; next year I will go out on the trawler for a week.' For five-year-old Troy all the aspirations, danced and spoken, look as unlikely to be fulfilled as the equivalent conversations we conduct between ourselves and our mirrors at thirty-five or fifty-five or, for all I know, ninety.

His younger sister arrives a pace behind. The first thing you notice about Lillit is her beauty. In the evenings, washed for bed in pink-flowered pyjamas, she is merely a preposterously pretty child. In the morning, amber flesh and golden eyes glowing through the grit and the snot-trails, she is an authentic beggar-maid princess. For all her beauty she's no narcissist. She has no interest in the magical mirror-door. Instead she watches her brother, and mimics his movements: a small, solid ghost, always a heartbeat behind, always implacably there, reducing warrior poses to charmingly vague flappings and fallings.

Perhaps he loves the door because it frees him from her stumpy reflection, an image he cannot find flattering. Last year she would stumble after his tricycle. This year he has a two-wheeler, so she runs. She runs with the peculiar shuffling run of the local children, feet flat, knees scarcely lifting. I think it comes from running in thongs. However far ahead he is she never gives up: way back on the dusty road there she is, steadily trotting. She always covers the course: even when he has lapped her, even when he is home again in their cubby among the roots of the big jacaranda, she trots on to the end of the road and the prescribed turn. It seems to be a matter of honour with her.

He mothers her because her mother doesn't, and he has embraced it as his duty. He is a good mother: if she falls he picks her up, dusts her down and delivers a brisk narrative of the catastrophe, nicely apportioning blame; if she bleeds he dabs the blood away and begs a bandaid from me. We know he must not bother his mother, who is a shrieker and hitter when roused.

I think he loves his sister. She is crucial to his expeditions, a Horatio responding like a strung bow to his ever-changing scenarios, a sturdy Sherpa cheerfully lugging the props. The first time I saw her she was struggling to push a toy wheelbarrow loaded with assorted paraphernalia through heavy sand, a great rope coiled around her neck, a bucket banging at her back, while her brother strolled ahead with his wooden sword. This year he has begun to reject her, theatrically, when his friends come around. They sit in their male semi-circle, knees drawn up to chins; he orders her out of the cubby-house; gratifyingly, she weeps and goes. The moment he stops actively driving her away, she is back, silent, radiant, infinitely pliable. She does not seem to know how to hold a grudge. It looks like an ideal relationship. I doubt he will ever be as happy with a woman again. After Lillit they will all fail him, one way or another.

As for Lillit, if her second characteristic is her devotion to her brother, I discover her third only when he is absent. She is a committed starer. She leans her hands against the table, her chest against her hands, widens her eyes to their amazing limit, and stares into your face with the lovely, limpid intensity of a baby calf. She does not care if you ignore her. She does not care if you eat or read or talk or sleep or pick your nose. She does not care if flies promenade across the shining expanses of her eyes. Lips parted, nose and mouth lightly dribbling—she is not only the most beautiful but the messiest child I have seen—she seems to be in the process of absorbing your entire being through those radiant surfaces. If your nerve cracks and you order her away she will go, but slowly, and backwards, a centimetre at a time, staring the while. There is no malice in her gaze, and no offence, either. She will stare at a lizard or a frog with precisely the same absorbed intensity—but never, I notice, for as long. You can get to the end of a lizard. Humans, it seems, are inexhaustible.

At first you mind and tell her to stop. After a while you get used to it. Another while, and you begin to stare back, and discover an archaic but curiously familiar pleasure, an atavistic balm for civilisation's woes. While the gaze is initially analytic—are those extraordinary eyes more golden or honey, is the pommette-flush more apricot or nectarine, is 'shell' the appropriate metaphor for that fondant ear with its melting pink lobe?—with time one sinks past the surfaces into a trance-like condition, a profound but impersonal intimacy which seems to well from some primordial source.

The sensation vaguely resembles post-coital repletion, but it is not in the least sexual. On the contrary: this is pre-lapsarian Eden, where we breathe and gaze and breathe again. Why has this pleasure been lost to us? Why has staring been declared impudent in children and menacing in adults? Mothers and babies stare at each other by the hour. Lovers eat each other with their eyes. The rest of us seem to have lost the knack of this most democratic form of intimacy, this secular grace, somewhere along the tangled paths of evolution. Man the lonely ape, the ape who has forgotten how to stare.

Lillit doesn't want a motorbike, she doesn't want to go out on the trawlers, she doesn't want to be older. She likes to have a pocket in her dungarees for the few things she thinks of as hers, but her attachment to these objects is slight: she gives them away or loses them with only formal regret. For the moment, she has everything that she wants: her brother, her share in the family dog, her almost silent songs which she sings as she stares. Physically she is tough, accepting injury nonchalantly unless there is advantage in tears. She is socially intrepid, dragging chairs to where she wants them, climbing up, leaning on the adults' table, thrusting her bald doll into the conversation. Deaf to adult exhortation, she is expert in intimate discourse, especially with males. Having listened with what looks like a parody of raptness to my husband's narrative of the events which must follow on her overbalancing—table, chair, child and doll all up-ended, child and doll weeping—she gazes, glows, and says, 'Then you will pick me up?' And teeters, deliciously.

With me she is different. She mimics me: moving to close the screen door a centimetre with exactly my look of conscious rectitude, digging holes for plants with actorish enthusiasm. This is for her own amusement. She has a very private sense of humour. Most of our conversation is direct woman-to-woman bargaining, she negotiating to extract more than her daily ration of one sweet, me struggling between my detestation of being manipulated and a grandmotherly passion to feed. Sometimes I yield, and then she is ruthless in advantage: in her view once makes a custom. Whatever the outcome she is always sunny. There are no hard feelings, just the battle renewed. She has the insouciance of those golden gods who signal to each other high above the grimy rooftops of decrepit Paris.

Obviously, I admire her. To tease me, and also because he believes it, my husband says that one day she will make some man a wonderful wife. I suppose she might. If she could marry her brother she would. But looking at her, thirty months in the world, and having measured the will behind the glowing face, I think I understand why men can fear women so much. Some day some man will come to depend on Lillit. He will come to live through and by and in her. He will come to take her for granted. But will it last? With Lillit I would always have the feeling that one day she might simply get up, and walk away.

NOW

Recuperating patients attend a post-transplant clinic, at first twice-weekly. On my first day I sat, nervous and deferential, on the edge of my chair, uncertain what to do, how to behave, feeling at once haughty and excluded. By morning's end I had been recruited into a society of a distinctive kind.

We are not really friends. We know too little of each other's lives beyond the hospital to be friends. What we are is comrades. We are like Roman veterans meeting back in the city between stints on the frontiers, serving in different camps, with the deprivations various, the natives differently troublesome, but sharing a knowledge incommunicable to all those others—family, lovers, friends—who know nothing of life on the frontier. The great dividers of class, occupation, faith, ethnicity, sex, age, have no authority here. The senior veterans command a touch more deference, that is all.

Not everyone is a member. Those people who, catapulted into sudden illness and emergency surgery, catapult as swiftly back to health do not belong. The children are not members. Prolonged debilitation seems to be a pre-condition for membership, and then experience of the slow, lurching waltz of recovery, step forward, step sideways, step together, step. We know that for us 'health' is an artificial condition. We will remain guinea pigs, experimental animals, for as long as we live. Or, if you prefer, angels borne on the wings of our drugs, dancing on the pin of mortality. We know that today is as contingent as tomorrow.

I think that is what we share. I cannot be sure because we do not talk about such things. We are content in one another's company, but I do not know if anyone felt and feels quite as I do, thought and thinks as I do.

I am back. That is how it seems to friends: the person they knew, the voice, the manner, the little box of social tricks, is back. And so she is. Except now I know more of the processes which made her, and therefore know her to be a fiction: a thing made out of idiosyncratically angled experiences and an obstinate habit of writing.

Late in the year of my transplant operation my husband and I built a house on an island in Far North Queensland—my third beach house. We built it partly to escape Melbourne winters, partly to mark a break with the past.

ISLAND

The old beach is too crowded now. There are too many ghosts. My mother steps neatly around a rockpool; my brother rummages in his old army bag, scowls; my sister sits hugging her knees, then runs down to the sea, knees turned in, feet flapping. A fat yellow dog lumbers into the water, chests the waves. My father is over there in the shallows, splashing his milk-pale shoulders and ochre wrists, then lowering himself slowly into the water. He takes a few strokes, scrabbles to find his feet, wades back to the shore, while we call from beyond the first line of breakers. I realise only now that he hated the sea. Why shouldn't he, a working-class boy from the city? Why shouldn't he hate the sea?

Then there are the ghosts of the living. A baby rides on a young man's shoulders. The man has a striped towel on his head; the baby whacks it with a spade. A silent hubbub, and a tide of boys swirls into a kitchen and out again, their hands crammed with food. Older, they play beach cricket into the night, until they are thin cries and white splashes, seabirds in the dark water. Then, suddenly, they are men, with wide necks and chests and shoulders. When I look at them, they look back.

I am there too: squatting in red dust watching the bull-ants; on a swing, hurtling higher than the pines to shoot feet first towards the sun, plunging back to the shadowed green; dancing with my shadow on the beach, feet stitched together, arms wild. I am seventeen, panting along the night beach, running from an angry man in a car; twenty-seven, dabbling a baby in a warm green pool; forty-seven, scratching the flaws on the skin of my thighs; fifty-seven, idling alone in the morning sea.

I have always hated photographs. I steal them if I can, tear them up, hide the pieces. Photographs steal your soul, photographs kill. The child will never smile that gap-toothed smile again; the dog in mid-leap is dead. The photographs in your head kill more slowly, layering the living flesh with other, earlier selves, other, earlier faces. My grandfather's irony tilts a son's mouth; a grand-niece looks at me with my sister's eyes. The ghosts are multiplying. Some days I can't see what is, for all the shadows in the way.

My husband and I go back to the old beach sometimes. We walk its length, note the familiar birds, the shells, privately wondering how we spent whole days there, turn back to the car, decide what to eat for dinner. Perhaps he saw the phantom figures, heard the voices, perhaps not. There's no point in discussing such things. We both chose to leave. We both chose the island.

It is different here. Here everyone is a stranger. We meet, nod, pass on. They sometimes say where they came from, where they once had been. Some are eager to talk, others not. We don't remember what they say, or we get it wrong—such things have no significance. We are not part of their story. They are local fauna: a colony of fluff-headed septuagenarians in flight from New Zealand's winter, a couple of stilt-legged Swedes, the sixty-year-old hippie in his draggled plumage stalking the beach.

The real birds matter more. Some are new to us. A pheasant-like creature teeters implausibly on a high branch; curlews are hallucinations by day, banshees by night; bee-eaters bright as hummingbirds spin through blue air. Others are dislocated variations of the familiar: if the colour is right the voice is wrong; if the voice is right there's a patch of yellow or a masked eye or an oddly undulant flight. Or familiar birds are in the wrong place. Spur-winged plovers work the sea edge, kookaburras gurgle in fan-palms. The images dance in our heads. We never tire of looking.

The beaches, too, are different. There are casuarinas instead of ti-trees, and solitary mangroves are hemmed with bright green lawns of shoots. The sand is wrong—too grey, too white, I don't know. Wrong. The rocks are huge grey elephants, big as bedrooms. They look as if they have walked from somewhere else, perhaps from inland or from another continent, another time. The flotsam crusting the shore is different. There's no plastic, more rope, the occasional whole tomato: yachties' litter. Crabs clump together in a stretch of sand. You hardly ever see them—a tremor in the corner of an eye like an indrawn breath, the sense of being watched—but they must come out sometimes, because they scribble all over the sand: doodles, arabesques, sometimes great hieroglyphs set in a carpet of fine-flocked sand. The hieroglyphs look Mayan, or perhaps Japanese.

And the shells, the shells are different. No beach has the same shells from one day to the next. Some days sand dollars are tossed up like Andromeda's apples, some days small dark cowries, some days flat blond whorls. Then they are gone, and there is something different. They say it's the way the reef currents run, or perhaps the dumpings of the prawners. I don't know why it happens. I'm a stranger here.

I have a garden of beansprouts in a yoghurt jar, and occasionally we hack at a fallen coconut, smug in its husk. That's the end of our housekeeping. The green tree ants weave their leaf houses by the terrace. Their abdomens taste of citron. We eat them with the flesh of prawns, and drop them in our drinks. We watch for turtles as the black wings of the trawlers brush the darkening water. We sleep well here.

I think we will never go back.

EPILOGUE

Of course we did come back from the island, which is another difference between fiction and life. I go to the clinic every couple of months, I count my pills, swallow them carefully. I intend to live.

What will I do with this gift of years? My technique for deciphering the hieroglyphs of my hallucinations was to explore my past with a professional historian's tenacity. In doing that I identified the experiences, often spread over years, which lay compacted behind certain insistent images, and uncovered connections previously unguessed at.

Then the task was urgent. It felt like life and death. Now both the energy and the desire to look further into the self are dead. I am tired of blundering about in the funhouse of the personal, with its multiplying images and its faces around corners. This stuck-together 'I' is tired of introspection, that interminable novel of the invention of the self. I am tired of the 'I', with its absurd pretensions to agency, so elegant, so upright, moving so serenely through the thickets of lesser words, surveying them from such a height. Poised on so narrow a base. It is difficult to take that preposterous pronoun seriously when you know it to be a fabricated, chemically supported, contingent thing.

I am not tired of history, because to be tired of history is to be tired of the world. It is also a refuge from one's own darker imaginings. People like Mr Robinson do not believe themselves to be fictions. They retain their faith in agency. They believe the stories they invent about themselves, and struggle to make them real. It is even possible that in different circumstances the Chief Protector might have prevailed.

As for fiction—Salman Rushdie says you need a lot of energy for fiction, and he is right. For a time I believed that broken dolls had no business playing with puppets. Now, as managing daily life becomes a less consuming project, as my drug-weighted spirits lighten, I sometimes find myself preoccupied with the affairs of imaginary creatures again.

I have dedicated this book to absent friends: to those people, most of them overseas but some of them here, who have been wondering what I have been doing this last long while. This is my explanation, my apology, and my greeting to you.

There are new friends made during this time out-of-time: the men and women of the medical, technical and general staff of the Austin Hospital at Heidelberg, Victoria, more especially the people associated with its Liver Transplant Unit, most especially Peter, Bob, Janet, Jenny, and a quiet housewife who turned out to be rather more courageous than Geronimo. It is a surprising thing to find oneself adopted into an affectionate family in late middle age, but that has been my privilege. These people saved my life and my sanity, a thing quickly said but impossible to grasp. Together with the family of my unknown donor, they have made me the gift of these last few years, and, if they have their way, of quite a few more to come. To them I say thank you.

I also thank Michael Heyward of Text Publishing. He is probably the only person in Australia who could have forced me to see the sense buried in what often seemed self-indulgent jottings.

Illness granted me a set of experiences otherwise unobtainable. It liberated me from the routines which would have delivered me, unchallenged and unchanged, to discreet death. Illness casts you out, but it also cuts you free. I will never take conventional expectations seriously again, and the clear prospect of death only makes living more engaging.

Illness also gave me a ringside seat at the continuing drama of Advanced Medical Science, which I find more exciting than any television melodrama, and more inspiriting than any sweaty sporting triumph. Having eyed it mistrustfully, I am now entranced by its intellectual audacity, its rigour, and the elegance of its diagnostic resolutions.

Illness also made me a writer. Through all its permutations I used writing to cling to the shreds of the self, and to sustain the fraying strands of memory connecting me to my past self, and to the people I love. It was also by way of illness, its enforced introspections and the analysis of its hallucinatory narratives, that I came to understand the depth of my commitment to doing history: to thinking systematically about why people think and act as they do.

The experience has also ratified my conviction that I, and therefore you, are unequivocally physical constructs, if spectacularly complicated ones.

So that is what I have been doing all this time—by courtesy of a physiological malfunction, taking a journey out, beyond and around myself, and into interior territories previously closed to me. At the end of it, battered, possibly wiser, certainly wearier and, oddly, happier, I have returned to where I began: to history, with a deepened sense of what peculiar creatures we are, you and I, making our marks on paper, puzzling over the past and the present doings of our species, pursuing our peculiar passion for talking with strangers.